Seated in Heavenly Places

Anne
McFee's

Ortenville

Cresent Rolls

M-15

Senior Lk
LAKAVILLE

24

Seated
in Heavenly
Places

by
Richard Booker

Destiny Image Publishers
P.O. Box 351
Shippensburg, PA 17257
717-532-3040

Also by Richard Booker
available from Destiny Image Publishers:

Come and Dine
Intimacy with God
Jesus in the Feasts of Israel
The Miracle of the Scarlet Thread
Blow the Trumpet in Zion
Radical Christian Living
How to Prepare for the Coming Revival

Scriptural quotations have been carefully selected from the following versions of the Bible:
KJV: King James Version
TLB: The Living Bible, © 1971 Tyndale House Publishers, Wheaton, IL. Used by permission.
RSV: Revised Standard Version
NKJ: The New King James Bible, © 1982 Thomas Nelson.

SEATED IN HEAVENLY PLACES

Destiny Image Publishers
P.O. Box 351
Shippensburg, PA 17257

ISBN 0-914903-73-X

For Worldwide Distribution

First Printing: 1986
Second Printing: 1989
Third Printing: 1992

Contents

Foreword

The Church of Jesus Christ suffers from an inadequate identity. The Church, the Body of Christ, is the most important, influential and powerful force in the universe outside of God himself. The world, and much of the Church, does not realize this. That is why it is not the most prestigious, although the most potent factor or agent, in all creation.

Although much of the Church has not understood its position, through Her God-given identity with Christ, God has given the Church power and authority over all the power of the enemy. (Luke 10:19)

When the Body of Christ fully appreciates the Lordship of Christ, continually walks in the Spirit, constantly ministers in the power of the Holy Ghost, persists in wearing the whole armour of God and living as Christ's follower or disciple, only then is this celestial power and authority available and effective.

In his book, *Seated in Heavenly Places,* Richard Booker has expounded some important Biblical secrets for exercising this power and authority.

Paul E. Billheimer

Acknowledgments

My love and gratitude to my wife, Peggy, for typing the manuscript and for living the abundant Christian life with me. I love you in Christ.

Thanks to Paul Billheimer for his kindness in writing the foreword. Paul is a dearly beloved man of God whose books have touched the hearts of people around the world. He went to be with our Lord in the early spring of 1984.

Thanks also to Danny Carpenter for his fine drawings.

1
The God-Kind Of Life

The cry of every human heart is to live a fulfilled and contented life free of the fear of want and death. In trying to obtain this life of contentment and immortality, we human creatures grasp for many straws that we think will help us find it. Some of the straws we grasp for are money, pleasure, power, prestige, fame, humanitarianism, self-gratification, freedom, accomplishments, security, greatness, friendship, etc. Whatever straw we are holding onto inevitably breaks. When this happens we reach out for another, and another and another. Before we realize it, our life is over, and instead of having contentment and immortality all we've got is a bunch of broken straws.

There is a person who claimed to be able to provide this life for us. This Person is Jesus Christ. Jesus said that He came that we might have life and that we might have it more abundantly. The apostle John recorded this statement by

1

Jesus in John 10:10. The Greek word that John used for life in this verse is "zoe." This word refers to the kind of life that comes only from God. It is the eternal life of God breathed into us so that we might live forever with Him.

Jesus said that He could and would give this eternal life to all who would come to Him. He can do this because He has this life within Himself and desires to share it with us. Jesus said this is an abundant life.

Whenever we come to Jesus, He shares this life with us by giving us the Holy Spirit of God. *Thus it is through the Holy Spirit that we receive and become partakers of the very life of God Himself.* When this God-kind of life controls us, we find fulfillment, contentment and freedom from the fear of want and death. We often speak of this as "life in the Spirit." This abundant life in the Spirit also enables us to have authority, power and victory over sin, Satan and eventually death itself. So you see, this is just the kind of life for which we are all looking. God's life is not like the broken straws of the world. And He will share it with anyone and everyone who will come to Him through Jesus Christ.

Why I Wrote This Book

I wrote this book to help you learn how to receive and enjoy this God-kind of life. You receive this life simply by turning from your sins and asking Christ to come and live in you through the Holy Spirit.

Now all Christians have received this God-kind of life. But unfortunately not all Christians are experiencing and enjoyings its full blessings. *The purpose of this book is to help you learn how to live in the God-kind of life in the Holy Spirit in the here and now.*

The Apostle Paul expressed my prayer for you as you read this book. He said, "I pray for you constantly, asking God, the glorious Father of our Lord Jesus Christ, to give you wisdom to see clearly and really understand who Christ is and all that he has done for you. I pray that your hearts will be flooded with light so that you can see something of the future he has called you to share. I want you to realize

2

that God has been made rich because we who are Christ's have been given to him! I pray that you will begin to understand how incredibly great his power is to help those who believe him. It is that same mighty power that raised Christ from the dead and seated him in the place of honor at God's right hand in heaven, far, far above any other king or ruler or dictator or leader. Yes, his honor is far more glorious than that of anyone else either in this world or in the world to come. And God has put all things under his feet and made him the supreme Head of the church—which is his body, filled with himself, the Author and Giver of everything everywhere" (Ephesians 1:17-23 TLB).

A Look At What's Ahead

You will begin in Chapter Two by learning that *God really does want you to have this abundant life in the Spirit.* You'll see that, through Jesus Christ, you have been given a position of authority and rule over the fear of want and death.

In Chapter Three, you will discover your *identification with Christ* in all that He has done on your behalf. What Jesus did in the flesh of His human body is available for you in your spirit. God considers you one with Christ in His crucifixion, burial, resurrection, ascension and exaltation. His victory in the flesh becomes your victory in the spirit.

Then in Chapter Four, you'll learn how to *appropriate Jesus as Lord of your life.* You see, Jesus did not come just to help us out when we get into trouble. He certainly does this and we appreciate it when He does. But He has something else much more wonderful in mind. He actually desires to live His own glorious life through us. So when we give our life completely to Him, His God-kind of life becomes real to us.

As you continue on to Chapter Five, you'll learn how to *live in this God-kind of life.* You can't actually live it yourself, but you can live in it. The Bible calls this "walking in the Spirit." As you walk in the Spirit, the very life of God is manifested to you and through you. The Holy Spirit

3

begins to live the character of Jesus Christ through you. The Apostle Paul spoke of this as the "fruit of the Spirit." The result is that your life will be filled with love, joy, peace, longsuffering, gentleness, goodness, faithfulness, meekness and temperance (self-control). This is truly an abundant life.

And there's even more. In Chapter Six you will learn how to *minister in the Spirit* in order to share this abundant life with others. God will give you power so that you can hear His voice, do His will and walk in His ways.

When you begin to minister in the Spirit, you soon encounter *spiritual warfare*. So in Chapter Seven, you'll become acquainted with your spiritual armor and learn how to use it to stand in the victory Jesus Christ has provided for you.

Finally, in Chapter Eight, you'll discover what it really means to *live as Christ's disciple*. You'll learn the real meaning of the word "disciple," how to be a disciple and the marks of true discipleship.

In addition, there is a *review exercise* at the end of each of the following chapters to help you highlight and reinforce what you have learned in the chapter. The review exercises may be completed on an individual or group basis. May God help you learn what it means to be *Seated in Heavenly Places*.

2
Knowing Your Dominion

When God made Adam He gave him *dominion, or rule, over planet earth.* We read in the book of Genesis, "And God said, Let us make man in our image, after our likeness: and let them have dominion over the fish of the sea, and over the fowl of the air, and over the cattle, and over all the earth, and over every creeping thing that creepeth upon the earth (Genesis 1:26 KJV).

God-Given Dominion

God had given Adam and Eve the title deed to planet earth. *They had a divine mandate and legal right to rule the earth for the glory of God.* But this right to rule was effective for Adam and Eve only as long as they lived in obedience and loving fellowship with God. They were in authority over everything on planet earth just as long as they themselves lived under God's authority.

5

Dominion Lost

But, as the Genesis account records, Satan tempted Adam and Eve to disobey God. (See Genesis 3.) And when Adam and Eve yielded to the temptation, they lost their position of rule and authority to Satan. The effect of this is that *Adam transferred the title deed of planet earth to Satan.* Satan then became the ruler and master of everything on planet earth, including Adam and Eve. Adam, therefore, not only lost the divine right to rule planet earth, but he himself came under the dominion of Satan.

The Rule Of Satan

Jesus spoke of Satan as the "prince of this world." (See John 12:31; 14:30; 16:11.) In 2 Corinthians 4:4, Paul referred to Satan as the "god of this world" (KJV). To the Ephesians, he spoke of Satan as the "prince of the power of the air" (Ephesians 2:2 KJV). John wrote that, "the whole world is in the power of the evil one" (1 John 5:19 RSV). In these and many other places in the Bible, *we learn that Adam and Eve and all of their descendants came under Satan's dominion.*

A Deadly Bondage

What does it mean to be under Satan's dominion? Basically it means that we become his slaves and must do whatever he tells us to do. The Bible tells us that the work of Satan is sin (1 John 3:8). Satan wants us to sin. He wants us to disobey God. And since we are under his authority, this is exactly what we do. The Bible says that all of us have sinned and the penalty for our sin is death (Romans 3:23; 6:23). Paul said it this way to the Romans, "Therefore, just as through one man sin entered the world, and death through sin, and thus death spread to all men, because all sinned" (Romans 5:12 NKJ). *All of Adam's descendants have inherited his slavery to Satan, his tendency toward sin and his fear of death.*

Now, of course, Satan doesn't tell us that we are his slaves. We wouldn't want to hear that, would we? That would make us very upset. Why? Because, in our pride, we like to think

6

we are our own person doing our own thing. So Satan lets us believe this, and we go through life serving him while thinking we are our own masters.

But the Bible says, "Nobody does their own thing." We're either doing God's thing or Satan's thing. We're either slaves to God or slaves to the devil. Paul wrote to the Romans, "Don't you realize that you can choose your own master? You can choose sin (with death) or else obedience (with acquittal). The one to whom you offer yourself—he will take you and be your master and you will be his slave" (Romans 6:16 TLB). Peter wrote "a man is a slave to whatever controls him" (2 Peter 2:19 TLB). Jesus said, "You are slaves of sin, every one of you" (John 8:34 TLB).

Even though we don't like to hear it, and most won't acknowledge it, we are all born into this world as slaves to Satan, slaves to sin and slaves to the fear of death. This is why we can't keep our New Year's resolutions. This is why we can't break the hold of self-destructive habits. This is why we are all afraid to die.

A Just Restoration

We've all got a problem. We need to be set free from this bondage. But our freedom must come in such a way that God's justice will not be violated. You see, God can't just suddenly change all the rules. God can't say to Satan, "Too bad, Satan. You've got to play by the rules, but I don't. So the deal is off. I'm giving it all back to Adam."

God must abide by His own laws of justice. *Dominion over the earth was given to man, and it was lost by man. Therefore, it can legally only be recovered by a man.*

But what man? As we've just learned, Adam and all of his descendants are slaves. And a slave has no legal standing. A slave cannot go into court and appeal his case. There is no offspring of Adam, no seed of man, who can take the case for us.

Yet, somehow, a human must be found on whom Satan has no claim, someone not in bondage to him, someone who can go into the courtroom of heaven and represent us, someone who can dismiss Satan's legal claim on us. *We need another Adam.* We need one who would be tempted just as the first Adam but who would not yield to the temptation. Therefore, he would be able to restore dominion, rule and authority to us.

The Promise Of Deliverance

And this is just what God promised He would provide for us. He gave this promise immediately after Adam and Eve sinned. This promise of a coming deliverer is recorded in Genesis 3:15. God is speaking to Satan through the serpent, and He says, "I will put enmity between you and the woman, and between your seed and her seed; he shall bruise your head, and you shall bruise his heel" (RSV).

Now this is a most interesting statement. God says to Satan that he will have a seed. This just means that Satan will have spiritual children who will be under his dominion and rule. *Satan's seed, or children, will be constantly at war with another seed whom God identifies as the seed of woman.*

God says this seed of woman is a he. Then He begins to talk about a continuous spiritual war between the seed of Satan and the seed of the woman. This war will eventually come down to a personal confrontation between the two. Satan will bruise the heel of the seed of the woman. This will be painful but not fatal. The seed of the woman will then recover and bruise the head of the serpent (Satan). The bruise to the head will be a fatal blow from which Satan will not be able to recover.

Now the curious part about this whole statement from God is His referral to the "seed of woman." *Whoever heard of a woman having her own seed?* That's not the way life is reproduced. The seed comes from man. But in this case, God says the one Who will deliver the fatal blow to Satan will come from the seed of woman.

8

The Virgin Birth

The Prophet Isaiah also spoke of this seed of woman. He said, "Therefore the Lord himself shall give you a sign; Behold, a virgin shall conceive, and bear a son, and shall call his name Immanuel" (Isaiah 7:14 KJV). The word Immanuel means "God with us."

Isaiah explained that the seed of woman refers to a virgin birth. He said that it would be God Himself coming to planet earth as a baby boy, born of a virgin. The virgin would not be the mother of God but would be the mother of the man God became. This son, born of a virgin, would be the one who would take dominion from Satan and restore it to us.

Now in the New Testament, we learn the identity of this seed of woman. We read the following in Matthew 1:18-25: "Now the birth of Jesus Christ was as follows: After His mother Mary was betrothed to Joseph, before they came together, she was found with child of the Holy Spirit. Then Joseph her husband, being a just man, and not wanting to make her a public example, was minded to put her away secretly. But while he thought about these things, behold, an angel of the Lord appeared to him in a dream, saying, 'Joseph, son of David, do not be afraid to take to you Mary your wife, for that which is conceived in her is of the Holy Spirit. And she will bring forth a Son, and you shall call His name JESUS, for He will save His people from their sins.' Now all this was done that it might be fulfilled which was spoken by the Lord through the prophet, saying, *'Behold a virgin shall be with child, and bear a Son, and they shall call His name Immanuel,'* which is translated, 'God with us.' Then Joseph, being aroused from sleep, did as the angel of the Lord commanded him and took to him his wife, and did not know her till she had brought forth her firstborn Son. And he called His name JESUS" (NKJ).

Paul also added this statement in his letter to the Galatians, "But when the fullness of the time had come, God sent forth His Son, born of a woman . . ." (Galatians 4:4 NKJ).

I hope you fully realize the significance of what we have

9

just read. These verses, along with many others, tell us that *Jesus Christ is the Creator-God, Who came to the earth as a man, born of a virgin, in order to destroy the power of Satan and restore dominion over planet earth to man.*

Jesus—The Seed Of Woman

Jesus had to be born perfect without sin as Adam was created perfect without sin. *This is why He could not be born of the seed of man.* If He had been born of the seed of man, He would have inherited Adam's sin nature passed down through his blood line. This would mean that Jesus would be Satan's slave just like the rest of us. Yet legally, according to God's justice, He had to be a real human to take our place. So quite logically, at least in God's mind, He was born of a virgin.

Now what human mind would ever think up "that" as a solution? Well, of course, none! No one would ever think of a virgin birth. And even if they did happen to stumble upon the idea, they sure wouldn't suggest it to anybody. They would be laughed out of town. Only God would come up with this solution. This is just one more proof that He is the real author of the Bible.

So Jesus was born perfect, without sin, as Adam was created perfect and without sin. *Through His own test of obedience similar to Adam's, Jesus would set us free from bondage to Satan, sin and the fear of death.* He would restore dominion over planet earth to all who would come to Him.

This is what Paul had in mind when he wrote, ". . . since by man [Adam] came death, by man [Jesus] came also the resurrection of the dead. For as in Adam all die, even so in Christ all shall be made alive. . . . And so it is written, The first man Adam was made a living soul; the last Adam [Jesus] was made a quickening spirit" (1 Corinthians 15:21-22, 45 KJV).

Dominion Challenged

Jesus is a man on whom Satan has no claim. He is a man who can legally and morally challenge Satan. He is another Adam.

10

This, of course, presents Satan with a real problem. He must figure out some way to get dominion over "this Adam" just as the first one. He must get this new Adam (Jesus) to rebel against God just as he did the first Adam. Satan becomes obsessed with this one scheme. He marshalls all of his demon forces and uses every bit of his cunning to get Jesus to sin.

We find this struggle of the ages coming face to face out in a hot desert. The two contestants are battling for dominion over man and planet earth. *Satan is tempting Jesus just as he did Adam in the garden.* But where Adam was in a perfect environment, Jesus was hot, tired, hungry and thirsty from forty days of fasting in the desert. He was vulnerable, and Satan knew it.

You can read about this clash in Matthew 4:1-11 (NKJ). This is what happened. Satan approached Jesus and said, "If You are the Son of God, command that these stones become bread." Now this is an interesting temptation. You see, no matter how hungry I am, I can't turn stones to bread. *But the Son of God can!* And Satan knew it. That's why he tempted Jesus in this way. Instead of yielding to the temptation, Jesus responded by telling Satan that, "Man shall not live by bread alone but by every word that proceeds out of the mouth of God."

But Satan didn't give up so easily. He tried again. This time he took Jesus up to the top of the temple, and said, Jesus, "if You are the Son of God, throw Yourself down [from the top of this temple]. For it is written: 'He shall give His angels charge concerning you,' and, 'In their hands they shall bear you up, lest you dash your foot against a stone.' " Again Jesus resisted the temptation and said, "It is written again, 'You shall not tempt the Lord your God.' "

Well, by then, Satan was discouraged, but he was not yet ready to give up. So he tried once again. He took Jesus to the top of a mountain and in a fleeting moment of time, flashed all the kingdoms of the world before Jesus. Then Satan said, Jesus, "All these things I will give You, if You will fall down and worship me."

11

With this temptation, Satan was offering Jesus the title deed to planet earth. But the price was to become Satan's slave just as with the first Adam. *Now Jesus did not question Satan's right to offer Him these kingdoms.* He knew that Adam had legally handed them over to Satan.

But once again, Jesus resisted the temptation and said, "it is written, 'You shall worship the Lord your God, and Him only you shall serve." Angels then came and ministered to Jesus. He then returned victoriously to Galilee in the power of the Holy Spirit.

Temptation In The Garden

But Satan was not about to give up. There was too much at stake. So he tried again in the garden of Gethsemane. Satan's temptation was so strong that Jesus agonized and He sweat great drops of blood from His forehead. There, all alone, Jesus as the Son of God cried out, "Father, if there's any way, take this cup from me."

In this cry of desperation, Jesus was looking ahead to the cross. *But He was thinking about more than His physical suffering.* He was thinking about His spiritual suffering. He was thinking about His soul being cut off from fellowship with His heavenly Father.

For the first time in all eternity, the unity between God the Father and God the Son would be broken. This is because Jesus would become sin for us. God's eyes are too holy and pure to even look upon sin. So Jesus knew that the Father would have to turn His face from Him. This is what Jesus was agonizing over. To bypass the cross was His greatest temptation. Yet He said, "Nevertheless, not my will Father, but yours be done." (See Matthew 26:36-46.)

Jesus Our Representative

Shortly afterwards the Roman soldiers came and took Jesus. After several mock trials and a number of horrible beatings, they crucified Him. *There on the cross and for the next three days and nights, Jesus annulled and reversed the consequences of the failure of Adam four thousand years*

12

earlier when he handed dominion over to Satan. Jesus experienced death and separation from the Father on our behalf. He took on our sins as He became our innocent substitutionary sacrifice. Isaiah prophesied this would happen and said, "Surely he hath borne our griefs, and carried our sorrows: yet we did esteem him stricken, smitten of God, and afflicted. But he was wounded for our transgressions, he was bruised for our iniquities: the chastisement of our peace was upon him; and with his stripes we are healed" (Isaiah 53:4-5 KJV).

The weight of all of our sins was more than Jesus could bear. So as the Son of Man (representative of all mankind) He cried out to God, "My God, my God, why have you forsaken me?" (See Matthew 27:46.) This was not a question but a cry of desperation and anguish as fellowship between Jesus and the Father was broken.

Finally, Jesus dismissed His spirit and died. They took His body down and put it in a burial tomb. *But His spirit and soul went to hell.* This was necessary because the penalty for sin is death. This is the physical and spiritual death. Spiritual death is separation from God. Jesus had to pay the full penalty for us. Paul wrote in Romans 8:32 that God spared not His own Son but delivered Him up for us all. (See Psalms 68:18, 88:6; Acts 2:31.)

Satan's Colossal Blunder

This was Satan's bruise to the heel of Jesus in fulfillment of Genesis 3:15. His heel was literally bruised as He pushed Himself up on the cross. But spiritually speaking, His heel was bruised as He was cut off from the Father and died as our sin substitute.

But in his frantic effort to tempt Jesus to sin, Satan made the most colossal blunder of all time. Here is where he went wrong. Since Satan had dominion over man, he had the power of death over man. A slave owner can kill his slaves if he so desires. Therefore, Satan had the legal right to destroy sinful man under his dominion. But Jesus had never sinned. Jesus was not under

13

his dominion. Therefore, Satan had no legal rights over Jesus.

So when Jesus allowed Satan to take His life, Satan became a murderer. He killed an innocent man. In God's justice, the penalty for murder is death. Now when a person is waiting on death row to be executed, he has no dominion over anybody. And so in Hebrews 2:14, it says that *Jesus, through His death, destroyed him* [*Satan*] *that had the power of death.*

Dominion Restored

So three days later, when some women went to where Jesus was buried, they were greeted by an angel who said, "Do not be afraid, for I know that you seek Jesus who was crucified. He is not here; for He is risen, as He said. Come, see the place where the Lord lay" (Matthew 28:5-6 NKJ). Jesus had risen because He had never sinned. Therefore death had no hold on Him.

After His resurrection, Jesus ascended to heaven where He presented His own blood as the legal evidence of Satan's guilt. *Then Jesus sat down on the throne of the universe showing that He has dominion over Satan, sin and death.*

The Apostle Paul wrote the Ephesians that God the Father has given Jesus a position "far above all principality, and power, and might, and dominion, and every name that is named, not only in this world, but also in that which is to come: And hath put all things under his feet . . ."(Ephesians 1:21-22 KJV).

He wrote to the Philippian Christians, "Therefore God also has highly exalted Him and given Him the name which is above every name, that at the name of Jesus every knee should bow, of those in heaven, and of those on earth, and of those under the earth, and that every tongue should confess that Jesus Christ is Lord, to the glory of God the Father" (Philippians 2:9-11 NKJ).

Peter wrote of Jesus "who has gone into heaven and is at the right hand of God, angels and authorities and powers having been made subject to Him" (1 Peter 3:22 NKJ).

Through His resurrection, Jesus delivered the final blow to Satan's head. And the good news is that His victory is ours. Paul said it this way to the Colossians, "And you, being dead in your trespasses and the uncircumcision of your flesh, He has made alive together with Him, having forgiven you all trespasses, having wiped out the handwriting of requirements [ordinances] that was against us, which was contrary to us. And He has taken it out of the way, having nailed it to the cross. Having disarmed principalities and powers, He made a public spectacle of them, triumphing over them in it" (Colossians 2:13-15 NKJ).

The Handwriting Of Ordinances

In these verses, Paul mentioned a document called the *handwriting of ordinances.* He says this handwriting of ordinances was against us. The handwriting of ordinances was also called a Certificate of Debt.

When criminals were put in jail in Rome, their crimes and the numbers of years penalty were listed and nailed to their cell door. Each year the jailer would go by the cell door and mark off the time served until the debt had been paid. This was the Certificate of Debt. It stayed nailed to the cell door until the debt was paid in full. Then the jailer would take the Certificate of Debt to the judge who would stamp it "paid in full." Then the prisoner would be set free.

This is what God has done for us through Jesus Christ. The handwriting of ordinances that was against us was all of our sins. We all have a Certificate of Debt bearing our name with our sins listed. The penalty for our sin is bondage to Satan, sin and death. *But God took that Certificate of Debt and nailed it to the cross of Jesus.* And when it was over, the Judge hanging on the cross cried out, "It is finished" (John 19:30). This was His victory cry. He meant that our sin debt had been paid in full. When we appropriate this payment in our own life, we are set free from the penalty and bondage of sin.

15

The Parade Of Triumph

Paul went on to say that Jesus disarmed or spoiled principalities and powers. The word "spoil" means to carry off as a captive. It refers to an ancient military practice. When a general conquered his enemy, a great homecoming parade would be given in his honor. This was called the *parade of triumph.* As the general came into the city, he would strip the opposing king, whom he had taken captive, of all his armor and march him down the main street as part of his parade. The whole city would turn out for the parade to cheer the general and celebrate the victory. Then they gave him the keys to the city.

Now this is just what Jesus has done for us. *He has disarmed Satan and taken him captive.* When He returned to heaven, God the Father had prepared a big homecoming parade for Him. It was the great parade of triumph. All the angels of heaven came out to meet Him. They joined together in singing, "Worthy is the Lamb who was slain to receive power and riches and wisdom and strength and honor and glory and blessing." Then God the Father gave Jesus the keys to death and hades (Revelation 1:18; 5:12 NKJ).

The great grip of fear that Satan has on people is the fear of death. *But the Christian no longer needs to fear death.* Jesus said, "I am the resurrection and the life. He who believes in Me, though he may die, he shall live. And whoever lives and believes in Me shall never die . . ." (John 11:25-26 NKJ).

Because of what Jesus has done for us, Paul wrote to the Corinthians, "O death, where is thy sting? O grave, where is thy victory? The sting of death is sin; and the strength of sin is the law. But thanks be to God, which giveth us the victory through our Lord Jesus Christ" (1 Corinthians 15:55-57 KJV).

Not only does the Christian have dominion over death, but *we also have dominion over Satan.* When we receive and walk in the God-kind of life in the Spirit, we are able to exercise authority over Satan. The Apostle John said it this way, "Ye are of God, little children, and have overcome them: because greater is he that is in you, than he that is in the world" (1 John 4:4 KJV).

Through the God-kind of life in the Spirit, *we also have power over sin.* Paul wrote to the Roman Christians, "For sin shall not have dominion over you . . ." (Romans 6:14 NKJ).

If you are a Christian, sin has no power over you, Satan has no authority over you and death cannot hold you. Paul summarized this with one grand statement, "Now thanks be to God who always leads us in triumph in Christ . . ." (2 Corinthians 2:14 NKJ).

Dear reader, you can join the parade of triumph by receiving Jesus Christ as your Lord and Savior. You can say to Satan, death and sin, "I know you seek (your name). That old man is not here. He is risen as a new creation in Christ."

In these next chapters, we are going to be learning how to walk in this triumph, how to walk in victory and how to walk in dominion. May God bless you as you continue in your reading.

Chapter 2—Knowing Your Dominion

Review Exercise 1

1. What was the effect of Adam and Eve's sin?

2. Why does the Bible refer to Jesus as the last Adam?

3. How did Jesus defeat Satan?

4. How can you apply this knowledge to your life?

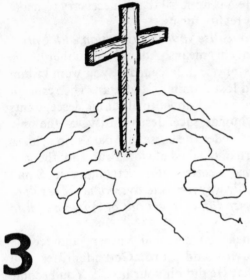

3
Identifying With Christ

The word "gospel" means good news. What we've just learned in the previous chapter is certainly good news. In fact, it's the greatest news in the world. *Jesus Christ has restored dominion to us so that we might have authority and power over Satan, sin, the fear of death and eventually death itself. This overcoming life is available to all who will give their life to Jesus Christ in order to receive His God-kind of life within him or herself.* Yet it's clear that many Christians are not experiencing the full blessings of this God-kind of life. One of the reasons is simply a lack of knowledge and understanding of the biblical principles that teach us how to live in this victorious Christian life. We are now going to begin to learn these principles.

Steps To Abundant Christian Living

I believe the Bible teaches three steps that we must take in order to enjoy the full blessings of the dominion Jesus has restored to us. These are steps that we must take by faith in God's Word that He has done all that is necessary to make this abundant life a reality for us.

The first step is to realize your identification with Christ. Let me explain what this means. Adam is the father of the human race. As his physical descendant, you were in him when he sinned and lost dominion to Satan. The result of this fall by Adam is passed down to all of his descendants which is the entire human race. Jesus Christ was the only person who was not under the curse of Adam's sin. This is because He was born of the seed of woman and not the seed of man. And He lived a perfect life, overcoming sin, Satan and death. *So the only way for us to overcome the result of Adam's fall, as Christ did, is to get out of Adam and into Christ.*

This happens when you personally accept and receive Christ as your Savior and Lord. God identifies you with Christ in all that He did on your behalf. You become one with Him. *What Jesus did in His flesh may be appropriated to your own life in the spiritual realm.* God makes this possible for us by placing us into spiritual union with Christ at the moment we receive His Spirit. Jesus spoke of this as being born again, or born from above. *It is a spiritual rebirth in which God takes us out of Adam and places us into Christ.* God explains this to us in the Bible by saying we have been crucified, buried, raised and seated with Christ in heavenly places. Now that's a pretty good place to be sitting. And the first step to experiencing the fullness of the Christian life is to realize this new life position you have in Christ.

The second step is to respond to His Lordship over your life. When you become a Christian, you give your life to Christ. This is a commitment in which you voluntarily die to yourself and hand over the rights to rule your own life to Jesus Christ. You recognize that your life now belongs to

Him. This is much like the relationship a young man desires to have with a young woman to whom he is attracted. He doesn't just want to be her friend. He wants to invade every area of her life. And so it is with Jesus Christ. *It is His desire to sit on the throne of your life and be the center of your universe.* And you must respond to His rule in order to live in His life.

The third step to experiencing the abundant Christian life is to walk in the Spirit. This simply means to allow the Holy Spirit to control your life. When you respond to the Lordship of Jesus, He will live His very own life out of you through the person of the Holy Spirit. This is the "zoe," or God-kind of life in the Spirit, that we mentioned in Chapter One. This is the overcoming life of Jesus Christ being lived out on planet earth in you through the Holy Spirit. *It is Christ in you living His own victorious life through you.*

So these are the three steps to living the abundant, victorious Christian life. In this chapter, we're going to examine the first step of realizing our identification with Christ. Then, in the remaining chapters, we'll learn about these others and how to take them.

Identifying With Christ

Paul gave us the best summary of our identification with Christ in the sixth chapter of his letter to the Romans. It would be helpful for you to really study that whole chapter. In this discussion we are going to consider verses 3-14.

In verse 3 Paul wrote, "Or do you not know that as many of us as were baptized into Christ Jesus were baptized into His death?" (Romans 6:3 NKJ).

In this chapter Paul was speaking to Christians. This is the "us" to whom he is referring. And he said that *every one of us who are Christians have been baptized into Jesus Christ.* This is a spiritual fact that Paul wanted us to know.

The word "baptized" means to be "put into," the result being that you are identified with and become one with that into which you are put. It is, in this instance, Christ. Sometimes people get confused and think Paul was talking about water baptism in these verses. This is because they haven't read Paul's words closely enough. In these verses, he said he was writing that we should realize our identification with Christ.

Now we've just mentioned that this spiritual identification or transaction takes place at the moment we ask Christ to come into our life. *He gives us the Holy Spirit Who joins us to Christ, placing us into spiritual union with Himself.* The two of us have become one spiritually. He is in you and you are in Him as a husband and wife become one in a physical union.

Paul said it in these words to the Corinthians, "For by one Spirit are we all baptized into one body, whether we be Jews or Gentiles, whether we be bond or free; and have been all made to drink into one Spirit" (1 Corinthians 12:13 KJV).

He wrote it this way to the Galatian Christians, "For as many of you as were baptized into Christ have put on Christ. There is neither Jew nor Greek, there is neither slave nor free, there is neither male nor female; for you are all one in Christ Jesus" (Galatians 3:27-28 NKJ).

So we see that being baptized into Christ means to be identified with Him in all He did on our behalf. Since this happens at the moment we put our trust in Christ and are saved, we often speak of this as baptism unto salvation. This spiritual transaction takes us out of Adam and establishes our new life position in Christ.

The Nature Of Our Identification

Now in verse 4, Paul explained how we are identified with Christ. He said, "Therefore we were buried with Him through baptism into death, that just as Christ was raised from the dead by the glory of the Father, even so we also should walk in newness of life" (NKJ).

Now let's examine Paul's statement. First, he said that we are identified with Christ in His *death*. When Jesus died, God saw us as having died with Him. Next, we are identified with Christ in His *burial*. God sees us buried with Christ. Then we are identified with Him in His *resurrection,* so that God sees us raised with Him. The purpose of this resurrection is that we should walk in newness of life. Finally, in Ephesians, Paul added the last aspect of our identification with Christ. He said we are *seated with Him* in heavenly places. (See Ephesians 2:5-6.)

Paul explained to the Ephesians that God, "even when we were dead in trespasses, made us alive together with Christ (by grace you have been saved), and raised us up together, and made us sit together in the heavenly places in Christ Jesus, that in the ages to come He might show the exceeding riches of His grace in His kindness toward us in Christ Jesus. For by grace you have been saved through faith, and that not of yourselves; it is the gift of God, not of works, lest anyone should boast. For we are His workmanship, created in Christ Jesus for good works, which God prepared beforehand that we should walk in them" (Ephesians 2:5-10 NKJ).

Crucified With Christ

Paul said in Romans 6:6 that our "old man" was crucified with Christ. Now who is this "old man" about whom Paul was speaking? *The old man is the sin nature that is within us.* When Paul spoke of sin in this chapter, he wasn't talking about the outward acts of sins we commit. He was talking about the self-centered rebellious nature within us that we inherited from Adam.

You see, we are not sinners because we sin; we sin because we're sinners. That is who we are. This old man, or sin nature within us, naturally loves to sin. *And as long as it is the ruling force in our life we will commit outward acts of specific sins.*

Jesus said it this way: ". . . from within, out of men's hearts, come evil thoughts of lust, theft, murder, adultery, wanting what belongs to others, wickedness, deceit, lewdness, envy, slander, pride, and all other folly. All these vile things come from within; they are what pollute you and make you unfit for God" (Mark 7:21-23 TLB).

23

Our problem is that we are born in Adam. And that's not a very good place to be. *We need to get out of Adam and into Christ.* Now some people try to do this by reforming themselves. They make New Year's resolutions, etc. They think they can break the hold that sin has on them by turning over a new leaf. But they soon learn they are not able to live up to their good intentions.

Paul spoke about this problem in Romans 7. He said, "I don't understand myself at all, for I really want to do what is right, but I can't. I do what I don't want to—what I hate. I know perfectly well that what I am doing is wrong, and my bad conscience proves that I agree with these laws I am breaking. But I can't help myself, because I'm no longer doing it. It is sin inside me that is stronger than I am that makes me do these evil things. I know I am rotten through and through so far as my old sinful nature is concerned. No matter which way I turn I can't make myself do right. I want to but I can't. When I want to do good, I don't; and when I try not to do wrong, I do it anyway. Now if I am doing what I don't want to, it is plain where the trouble is: sin still has me in its evil grasp. It seems to be a fact of life that when I want to do what is right, I inevitably do what is wrong. I love to do God's will so far as my new nature is concerned, but there is something else deep within me, in my lower nature, that is at war with my mind and wins the fight and makes me a slave to the sin that is still within me. In my mind I want to be God's willing servant but instead I find myself still enslaved to sin. So you see how it is: my new life tells me to do right, but the old nature that is still inside me loves to sin. Oh, what a terrible predicament I'm in! Who will free me from my slavery to this deadly lower nature? Thank God! It has been done by Jesus Christ our Lord. He has set me free" (Romans 7:15-25 TLB).

Does that sound familiar? God says the solution is not to turn over a new leaf but a new life. The old Adam-like nature cannot be reformed. It must be killed. And the good news is that God has killed it by nailing it to the cross of Jesus Christ.

Paul said that the reason God did this was so that the body of sin might be destroyed (Romans 6:6). He was talking about our physical body being enslaved to that sin nature within us. The result is that we think evil thoughts with our mind. We lust with our eyes. We speak evil with our tongue. We listen to foul talk with our ears. We strike someone with our hand.

Our body responds to the Adam-like nature within us through outward acts of sin. But if the Adam-kind of life within us has been crucified with Christ, our body no longer has to serve it. So Paul said that when our old man was crucified with Christ, that Adam-like nature was destroyed. The word "destroyed" does not mean "annihilated," but it means to be made powerless. *When our old man was crucified with Christ, its power over us was broken.* Therefore, we do not have to serve sin.

A person who has been crucified has no power over anyone. Have you ever see a dead person sin? But why do Christians, whose old man has been crucified with Christ, continue to sin? One of the main reasons is because they do not realize their identification with Christ. This is why Paul said, three times in these verses, that this is what he wanted us to know. He wanted you to understand that, when you give your life to Him, you become one with Christ in all that He has done for you.

Buried With Christ

Not only were you crucified with Christ, but you were also buried with Him. When Jesus died, they took His body down and placed it in a borrowed tomb. His body was in that tomb for three days and three nights. *God sees your old man buried with Jesus in that same tomb.*

During that time, though many Christians do not realize this, His spirit and soul went to hell. (See Psalms 16:10, 68:18; 88:6; Acts 2:27, 31.) This was required in order for Jesus to pay the full penalty of sin for us. This penalty is death to the body and death to the soul. Death to the soul is separation from God in hell. God sees your spirit and soul separated from Him in hell through Christ.

God sees us in Christ each step of the way as He paid the penalty of sin for us. We were there because we are in Him. That's why we don't have to pay the penalty for sin ourselves. Jesus has already paid it for us. That's why you don't have to go to hell. Jesus has already been there in your place.

Raised With Christ

But Jesus' body didn't stay in the tomb, and His soul and spirit didn't stay in hell. Because Jesus never sinned, death and hell couldn't hold Him (Acts 2:22-36). So, after three days and three nights, Jesus came forth from the dead in resurrection power. *And you too have come forth in resurrection power in your spirit because you were in Him.*

This is what Paul meant when he wrote to the Corinthians, "Therefore if any man be in Christ, he is a new creature: old things are passed away; behold, all things are become new" (2 Corinthians 5:17 KJV). *We who were dead in our trespasses and sins were raised up with Christ in our spirit-man to walk in newness of life victorious over sin, Satan and the fear of death.*

Paul summarized all of this with these words, "I have been crucified with Christ; it is no longer I who live, but Christ who lives in me; and the life I now live in the flesh I live by faith in the Son of God, who loved me and gave himself for me" (Galatians 2:20 RSV).

Realizing Your Position

These are wonderful spiritual truths to know, but how do we apply them to our lives on a daily basis? We apply them by simply realizing they are true and living within that realization. Here's how Paul said it to the Romans, "Likewise you also, reckon yourselves to be dead indeed to sin, but alive to God in Christ Jesus our Lord. Therefore do not let sin reign in your mortal body, that you should obey it in its lusts. And do not present your members as instruments

26

of unrighteousness to sin, but present yourselves to God as being alive from the dead, and your members as instruments of righteousness to God. For sin shall not have dominion over you, for you are not under law but under grace" (Romans 6:11-14 NKJ).

In verse 11, Paul used the word "reckon." This means simply to regard or consider your identification with Christ as truth and live accordingly. *Since your old Adam-like nature was crucified and buried with Christ, it no longer has power over your body. Since Christ was raised from the dead, you too have been raised in your spirit-man. You now have the God-kind of life in you. The God-kind of life in you is more powerful than your old man. Therefore, you don't have to be a slave to sin. You don't have to yield your body and its members to that old man. You have been freed from its sinful hold on you!*

Now you can freely yield your body to God. Your body can be an instrument of righteousness. For example, you can think with the mind of Christ. You can use your ears to hear the Word of God, your eyes for love rather than lust, your hands to give a cold drink of water, your feet to carry this good news to others. Sin shall not have dominion over you, but you shall have dominion over sin.

This doesn't mean that you are never going to sin again. The Apostle John clarified this for us. He wrote, "If we say that we have no sin, we deceive ourselves, and the truth is not in us. . . . If we say that we have not sinned, we make him a liar, and his word is not in us" (1 John 1:8, 10 KJV).

John seemed to contradict himself later in this same letter. He said, "Whosoever is born of God doth not commit sin; for his seed remaineth in him: and he cannot sin, because he is born of God" (1 John 3:9 KJV). The Greek word translated into English as "commit" means "to keep on committing." It doesn't mean that you will never sin. It means you won't make it your practice. You won't keep on committing sin as your life style.

The Living Bible says it so clearly with these words, "The person who has been born into God's family does not make a practice of sinning, because now God's life is in him; so he can't keep on sinning, for this new life has been born into him and controls him—he has been born again" (1 John 3:9 TLB).

It seems, for many Christians, that defeat is the routine while the victory is the exception. *Knowing and acting on your identification with Christ reverses this situation.* The victory will become the routine and the defeat will become the exception. You won't be perfect, but you will be different. I like to say it this way, "I'm not what I want to be, and I'm not what I'm going to be, but praise God, I'm not what I used to be!"

Seated With Christ

Not only do you as a Christian have dominion over sin, but you also have dominion over Satan. Jesus was not only raised from the dead; He was also exalted at the right hand of the Father where he is now sitting on the throne of the universe.

Paul wrote to the Ephesians that God raised Jesus from the dead "and seated Him at His right hand in the heavenly places, far above all principality and power and might and dominion, and every name that is named, not only in this age but also in that which is to come. And He put all things under His feet, and gave Him to be head over all things to the church, which is His body, the fullness of Him who fills all in all" (Ephesians 1:20-23 NKJ).

Jesus is on the throne of the universe. This means that He has rule and authority and power over sin, Satan, and death. Paul said that Jesus is also the head of the Church, which is His body. Every Christian has been joined to Christ by the Holy Spirit. First Corinthians 6:17 reads, "But he who is joined to the Lord is one spirit with Him" (NKJ).

Jesus is the head of a company of people who have been placed into spiritual union with Him. The Bible calls this company of people the Church. We are members of His body, having an organic union with Him as our head.

28

Now wherever your head is, your body is also. *Since you are in Christ and joined to Him spiritually, wherever He is, you are.* Since He is seated on the throne, where do you think you are seated? If you said, "on the throne," you answered perfectly.

Here's how Paul said it to the Ephesians, "And you he made alive, when you were dead through the trespasses and sins in which you once walked, following the course of this world, following the prince of the power of the air, the spirit that is now at work in the sons of disobedience. Among these we all once lived in the passions of our flesh, following the desires of body and mind, and so we were by nature children of wrath, like the rest of mankind. But God, who is rich in mercy, out of the great love with which he loved us, even when we were dead through our trespasses, made us alive together with Christ (by grace you have been saved), and raised us up with him, and made us sit with him in the heavenly places in Christ Jesus" (Ephesians 2:1-6 RSV).

Paul reminded us that at one time we were dead in our trespasses and sins. We walked according to the prince of the power of the air (Satan). By this he means we were under Satan's dominion. But now we have dominion over Satan because of our new life position in Christ.

A Divine Transplant

Paul wrote to the Colossians that God has "delivered us from the power of darkness [Satan], and hath translated us into the kingdom of his dear Son" (Colossians 1:13 KJV). The word "translate" refers to an ancient practice of warfare. When a king would conquer a country, he would move the conquered people from their own country to his country, or to another country he had conquered. This involved a mass relocation of the population. In the year 721 B.C., when the king of Syria conquered the ten northern tribes of Israel, he relocated the people to his own land (2 Kings 17). They came under his dominion, rule and authority.

Likewise, Jesus has conquered Satan. And, spiritually speaking, He has taken us away and relocated us. We no longer live under Satan's rule. We have been relocated into the Kingdom of Christ. Although physically we are still on planet earth, spiritually we sit with Christ in heavenly places.

Jesus is our King. We have been joined to Him in the spirit. His authority and power is ours. Therefore, we rule with Him with dominion over sin, Satan, the fear of death, and eventually death itself. This is what Jesus meant when He said, ". . . the kingdom of God is within you" (Luke 17:21 KJV).

Paul told the Philippian Christians that they were a colony of heaven on planet earth. He had this in mind when he wrote the Colossians, "If then you were raised with Christ, seek those things which are above, where Christ is, sitting at the right hand of God. Set your mind on things above, not on things on the earth. For you died and your life is hidden with Christ in God. When Christ who is our life appears, then you also will appear with Him in glory" (Colossians 3:1-4 NKJ).

The Final Victory

The final victory for the Christian is victory over death. Since death had no dominion over Christ, neither does it have dominion over those who are in Christ. Paul wrote to the Corinthians, "Now if Christ is preached that he has been raised from the dead, how do some among you say that there is no resurrection of the dead? But if there is no resurrection of the dead, then Christ is not risen. And if Christ is not risen, then our preaching is vain and your faith is also vain. Yes, and we are found false witnesses of God, because we have testified of God that He raised up Christ, who He did not raise up—if in fact the dead do not rise. For if the dead do not rise, then Christ is not risen. And if Christ is not risen, your faith is futile; you are still in your sins! Then also those who have fallen asleep in Christ have perished. If in this life only we have hope in Christ, we are of all men the most pitiable. But now Christ is risen from the dead, and has become the firstfruits of those who have fallen asleep. For since by man came death, by Man also came the resurrection of the dead. For as in Adam all die, even so in Christ all shall be made alive. But each one in his own order: Christ the firstfruits, afterward those who are Christ's at His coming. Then comes the end, when He delivers the kingdom to God the Father, when He puts an end to all rule and all authority and power. For He must reign till He has put all enemies under His feet. The last enemy that will be destroyed is death" (1 Corinthians 15:12-26 NKJ).

Some of the religious leaders of Paul's day were teaching that there was no resurrection of the dead. Paul argued, "If there's no resurrection, then Christ didn't rise from the dead. If Christ didn't rise from the dead, then we have no hope. Our faith in the resurrection of Christ is of no value. We might as well eat, drink and be merry for tomorrow we die."

But Paul declared that Christ is risen from the dead. He is the firstfruits from the dead. "Firstfruits" is an agricultural term. The farmer would go into his field and check the firstfruits of his harvest. *If he accepted the firstfruits, he would also accept the rest of his harvest.* God the Father accepted Jesus as the firstfruits from the dead. Since He was accepted, so we too will be accepted.

Because of this hope, the Bible doesn't speak of Christians as dying. It says we sleep. Our bodies go into the ground and our spirit and soul go to heaven there to await the resurrection of the body. Paul wrote to the Corinthians that to be absent from the body was to be present with the Lord (2 Corinthians 5:8).

First Corinthians 15:51-58 reads, "Behold, I tell you a mystery: We shall not all sleep, but shall all be changed— in a moment, in the twinkling of an eye, at the last trumpet. For the trumpet will sound, and the dead will be raised incorruptible, and we shall be changed. For this corruptible must put on incorruption, and this mortal must put on immortality. So when this corruptible has put on incorruption, and this mortal has put on immortality, then shall be brought to pass the saying that is written: *'Death is swallowed up in victory.' 'O death, where is your sting? O Hades, where is your victory?'* The sting of death is sin, and the strength of sin is the law. But thanks be to God, who gives us the victory through our Lord Jesus Christ. Therefore, my beloved brethren, be steadfast, immovable, always abounding in the work of the Lord, inasmuch as you know that your labor is not in vain in the Lord" (NKJ).

We also learn in Paul's letter to the Thessalonian Christians, "But I do not want you to be ignorant, brethren, concerning those who have fallen asleep, lest you sorrow as others who have no hope. For if we believe that Jesus died and rose again, even so God will bring with Him those who sleep in Jesus. For this we say to you by the word of the Lord, that we who are alive and remain until the coming of the Lord will by no means precede those who are asleep. For the Lord Himself will descend from heaven with a shout, with the voice of an archangel, and with the trumpet of God. And the dead in Christ will rise first. Then we who are alive and remain shall be caught up together with them in the clouds to meet the Lord in the air. And thus we shall always be with the Lord. . . . For God did not appoint us to wrath, but to obtain salvation through our Lord Jesus Christ, who died for us, that whether we wake or sleep, we should live together with Him. Therefore comfort each other and edify one another, just as you also are doing" (1 Thessalonians 4:13-17; 5:9-11 NKJ).

When Lazarus died, his sister came to Jesus for comfort. John recorded the following conversation: "Then Martha said to Jesus, 'Lord, if You had been here, my brother would not have died. But even now I know that whatever You ask of God, God will give you.' Jesus said to her, 'Your brother will rise again.' Martha said to Him, 'I know that he will rise again in the resurrection at the last day.' Jesus said to her, 'I am the resurrection and the life. He who believes in Me, though he may die, he shall live. And whoever lives and believes in Me shall never die. Do you believe this?' " (John 11:21-26 NKJ).

Jesus Christ is going to return to planet earth and give a new glorified body to all who are in Him. It will be a body just like His. Job said it for all of us with these words, "For I know that my redeemer liveth, and that he shall stand at the latter day upon the earth: And though after my skin worms destroy this body, yet in my flesh shall I see God: Whom I shall see for myself, and mine eyes shall behold, and not another; though my reins be consumed within me" (Job 19:25-27 KJV).

If you don't know Christ as your Savior and Lord, I pray that you will invite Him into your life right at this moment. *Knowing Christ personally is the only way you will ever be able to overcome the temptations to sin, the snares of Satan and the fear of death.* If you know Christ, realize your identification with Him so that you may live in His God-kind of life in the Spirit.

Chapter 3—Identifying With Christ

Review Exercise 2

1. List the three steps to abundant Christian living.
   a.

   b.

   c.

2. What does it mean to be identified with Christ?

3. List the four aspects of our identification with Christ.
   a.

   b.

   c.

   d.

4. What does it mean to be seated with Christ in heavenly places?

5. How can you apply this knowledge to your life?

4

Appropriating His Lordship
(take)

In the previous chapter I mentioned three steps we must take in order to enjoy the full blessings of the Christian life. The first step, as you have just learned, is to realize your identification with Christ. The second step, which you are now going to learn about, is to appropriate the Lordship of Jesus in your life. This just simply means to recognize God's claim on your life as a Christian and respond to His will for your life in loving trust and obedience.

It is absolutely necessary to have an understanding of the Lordship of Jesus Christ. So we're going to begin this chapter by recognizing and acknowledging that Jesus is Lord, and then we'll look into five aspects of His Lordship and how they affect our life.

Jesus Is Lord

In the Psalms David wrote, "The LORD said unto my Lord, Sit thou at my right hand, until I make thine enemies thy footstool" (Psalm 110:1 KJV). Notice that in this quotation, the first use of the word "Lord" is in capital letters. The second mention of the word "Lord" is in lowercase letters.

There is a reason for this. The Jews were afraid to actually say the name of God for fear of speaking His name irreverently. So instead of saying "Jehovah," which is the English transliteration of the Hebrew name YHWH, they would just refer to God as "Lord." But this presents a problem, because the word "Lord" actually refers to God's position as the ruler over all His creation. *They had to have some way of distinguishing when they were referring to God's name and when they referred to His position.* His name is Jehovah; His position is Lord. He is Jehovah the Lord. So when the Bible was translated into English, the translators put the word "LORD" in capital letters when they were referring to God's name, and they put the word "Lord" in lowercase letters when they were referring to His position.

Now the interesting part about all of this becomes obvious when we examine David's statement. The first use of the word "LORD" refers to God's name (Jehovah). The second use of the word "Lord" refers to His position as ruler of the universe. Jehovah God speaks to David's Lord and says, "Sit at my right hand until I make your enemies your footstool." God is going to sit David's Lord at His own right hand and give Him rule, authority, and power. David's Lord will rule as King of kings and Lord of lords from the very throne of God. Therefore, He will rule with all authority and all power.

A Divine Riddle

Jesus claimed that He was the one about whom this verse was speaking. He referred to it to show the religious leaders how little they really understood the Scriptures. They knew the Scriptures, but they didn't understand them because their hearts were evil.

Matthew gave us the following account, "While the Pharisees were gathered together, Jesus asked them, saying, 'What do you think about the Christ? Whose Son is He?' They said to Him, 'The Son of David.' He said to them, 'How then does David in the Spirit call Him "Lord," saying: "The LORD said to my Lord, 'Sit at My right hand, Till I make Your enemies Your footstool' "? If David then calls Him "Lord," how is He his Son? And no one was able to answer Him a word, nor from that day on did anyone dare question Him anymore" (Matthew 22:41-46 NKJ).

Jesus had the religious leaders acknowledge that the Christ (Messiah) was to be the Son of David. *Then He asked them how was it that David could call his own son "Lord."* They couldn't answer Jesus' question. They didn't know how the Messiah could be David's son as well as his Lord. To put it another way, "How could David's Lord also be his son?"

Jesus explained this divine riddle for us in Revelation 22:16. He said, "I am the root and the offspring of David . . ." (KJV). By this Jesus meant He was both before David and after David. But how can this be? Well, Jesus was before David because He is God. He is the Creator of the universe and the author and source of all life. (See John 1:1-4; Colossians 1:16-17; Hebrews 1:2-3; Acts 17:28.) Since all things were made by Him, He is the root of David. David actually came out of Him. But when God prepared for Himself a body and came to the earth, He did so in the womb of a woman who was of the lineage of David. So, as Jesus the man, He is the offspring of David.

The Prophet Isaiah tied all of this together when he wrote, "For unto us a child is born, unto us a son is given: and the government shall be upon his shoulder: and his name shall be called Wonderful, Counsellor, The mighty God, The everlasting Father, The Prince of Peace" (Isaiah 9:6 KJV).

Jesus Proves He Is Lord

After Jesus was resurrected, He told His followers that he was going to the Father. And when He went to the Father,

37

He was going to sit at His right hand. He would sit on the throne of the universe and rule with all authority and power. Anticipating this, Jesus said, "All authority has been given to Me in heaven and on earth" (Matthew 28:18 NKJ).

Jesus now sits at the right hand of God the Father as King of kings and Lord of lords. (See Acts 2:30; Revelation 3:21; 21:5.) But how do we know this? Is it just blind faith? No, it's not blind faith. *We can know this because Jesus has sent the Holy Spirit as proof to our hearts and minds that Jesus is Lord.*

We find this evidence of His Lordship being manifested on the day of Pentecost. This was a Jewish holy day; tens of thousands of Jews had journeyed to Jerusalem to celebrate the event.

At the same time, a company of about 120 of Jesus' followers were waiting for Jesus to send them the Holy Spirit as He had earlier promised (Luke 24:49; Acts 1:4). *This would be their proof that He really had ascended to the throne of God and taken His position as Lord of the universe.*

Luke recorded what happened that day. He wrote, "Now when the Day of Pentecost had fully come, they were all with one accord in one place. And suddenly there came a sound from heaven, as of a rushing mighty wind, and it filled the whole house where they were sitting. And there appeared to them divided tongues, as of fire, and one sat upon each of them. And they were all filled with the Holy Spirit and began to speak with other tongues, as the Spirit gave them utterance. Now there were dwelling in Jerusalem Jews, devout men, from every nation under heaven. And when this sound occurred, the multitude came together, and were confused, because everyone heard them speak in his own language. Then they were all amazed and marveled, saying to one another, 'Look, are not all these who speak Galileans? And how is it that we hear, each in our own language in which we were born?' " (Acts 2:1-8 NKJ).

These Jews had come from many different countries to celebrate the Feast of Pentecost. And while they were all in

Jerusalem, Jesus sent the Holy Spirit upon His followers. When this happened, they began to worship Jesus as Lord in the tongues and languages of the Jews. The Jews heard this and came to see what was taking place. They were astonished that these Galilean followers of Jesus were speaking in their own native languages.

Peter Presents The Evidence

When they gathered around to listen, Peter stood up to preach. As part of his sermon, he said, "This Jesus God has raised up, of which we are all witnesses. Therefore being exalted to the right hand of God, and having received from the Father the Promise of the Holy Spirit, He poured out this which you now see and hear" (Acts 2:32-33 NKJ).

Peter then quoted the passage from Psalms and said, "For David did not ascend into the heavens, but he says himself: 'The LORD said to my Lord, "Sit at My right hand, Till I make Your enemies Your footstool" ' " (Acts 2:34-35 NKJ).

Peter then applied this verse to Jesus and said, "Therefore let all the house of Israel know assuredly that God has made this same Jesus, whom you have crucified, both Lord and Christ" (Acts 2:36 NKJ). *Jesus Christ is Lord.*

We are now going to consider five aspects of His Lordship and see how they apply to our lives today.

Jesus—Lord Over Nature

First of all, Jesus is Lord over *nature*. Jesus demonstrated this many times in the Bible. One occasion is recorded for us in the eighth chapter of Matthew. The scene was in the town of Capernaum on the sea of Galilee. A great crowd had come to hear Jesus talk. In order to get away from the crowd, Jesus went to the other side of the sea.

Calm In The Storm

But as Jesus and His disciples made their way across the sea, there arose a great storm. The waves were about to sink the boat. So the disciples bailed out water just as fast as they could. But it was a losing battle. The boat was going to sink.

39

Interestingly enough, *Jesus slept through the whole storm.* It didn't bother Him at all!

Finally, as they were about to sink, the disciples woke Jesus up. Matthew gave us the following account, "Then His disciples came to Him and awoke Him, saying, 'Lord, save us! We are perishing!' But He said to them, 'Why are you fearful, O you of little faith?' Then He arose and rebuked the winds and the sea. And there was a great calm. And the men marveled, saying, 'Who can this be, that even the winds and the sea obey Him?' " (Matthew 8:25-27 NKJ).

The disciples were asking the question that people have been asking for the last two thousand years: Who is Jesus Christ? They may not have known exactly who Jesus was, but they knew from this experience that Jesus was Lord over nature. The wind and the sea obeyed Him.

Walking On Water

On another occasion, Jesus demonstrated His Lordship over nature by walking on the water. He had just miraculously fed the five thousand with the five loaves of bread and two fish. Once again He sent His disciples across the Sea of Galilee. Again, there was a storm. The winds were so strong that the disciples, though they rowed far into the night, had only gone a few miles.

Matthew said that Jesus then came out to them walking on the water. Of course, the disciples were terrified when they saw Him. They thought He was a ghost. But Peter got out of the boat and began to walk on the water towards Jesus. But when Peter realized what he was doing, he became afraid and began to sink. Jesus rescued Peter and helped him to the boat. The wind stopped, and they all worshiped Jesus and acknowledged Him as the Son of God. (See Matthew 14:22-23.)

In these and many other episodes, Jesus demonstrated that He was Lord over nature. As the writer of Hebrews put it, *Jesus holds all of nature together by the power of His spoken word* (Hebrews 1:3). And any time He desires, He can command nature to obey Him.

40

Jesus—Lord Over Life And Death

Jesus also claimed and demonstrated that He is Lord over life and death. Jesus said to the Jews, "Most assuredly, I say to you, he who hears My word and believes in Him who sent Me has everlasting life, and shall not come into judgment, but has passed from death into life. Most assuredly, I say to you, the hour is coming, and now is, when the dead will hear the voice of the Son of God; and those who hear will live. For as the Father has life in Himself, so has He granted to the Son to have life in Himself" (John 5:24-26 NKJ).

Jesus claims that He has life in Himself. Therefore He has authority over life and death. On another occasion, Jesus said, "Therefore My Father loves Me, because I lay down My life that I may take it again. No one takes it from Me, but I lay it down of Myself. I have power to lay it down, and I have power to take it again . . ." (John 10:17-18 NKJ).

Life To A Little Girl

Jesus demonstrated His authority over life and death by raising the dead. There was a ruler of the synagogue named Jairus. Jairus had a twelve-year-old daughter who, I'm sure, was the delight of her daddy's heart. But she got sick and was near death.

Now Jairus had heard of Jesus' miracles. So he sought out Jesus and asked Him to come and pray for his little girl before it was too late. Jesus agreed to go and pray for the girl. But as they went towards Jairus' house, one of his servants met them with bad news. He told Jairus that his daughter was dead. *Jesus comforted Jairus by telling him not to be afraid, just believe and the girl would be healed.* So they went on to the house. By the time they arrived, the funeral mourners and music had already started. Jesus told them to stop mourning for the girl was not dead, but only asleep. (He really knew that she was dead, but to Him she was nothing more than asleep.) They laughed at Jesus' statement. But He dismissed them, went into the room where the girl was lying and commanded life to return to her body. Immediately the girl sat up. Jesus then made a

41

mockery out of death by telling the bystanders to give her something to eat. By that time they weren't laughing anymore. (See Luke 8:40-56.)

Life To A Widow's Son

On another occasion, Jesus went to a city called Nain. As He entered the city, He was met by a funeral procession. A widow's only son had died. Now they were carrying his body on a funeral bed outside the city to place it in a tomb. A great crowd was following the funeral procession.

Jesus touched the funeral bed and the pallbearers stopped. They weren't sure that He was doing to say or do. With a show of compassion and power, Jesus commanded life to return to the young man's body. Immediately he sat up on his funeral bed. Of course this scared everyone, and they began to glorify God and give praise to Jesus. (See Luke 7:11-17.)

Life To A Friend

The third person whom Jesus raised from the dead was his friend Lazarus. Lazarus had become sick and died. By the time Jesus arrived he had been dead for four days.

This prompted the following conversation between Martha, Lazarus' sister, and Jesus: "Martha said to Him, 'I know that he will rise again in the resurrection at the last day.' Jesus said to her, 'I am the resurrection and the life. He who believes in Me, though he may die, he shall live. And whoever lives and believes in Me shall never die. Do you believe this?' She said to Him, 'Yes, Lord, I believe that You are the Christ, the Son of God, who is come into the world' " (John 11:24-27 NKJ). Jesus then went to Lazarus' tomb and called him forth from the dead.

Life To All

These three raisings of the dead were to prepare the people for the great resurrection of Jesus.

It was the first day of the week when the women went to His tomb. An angel greeted them and said, "Do not be afraid, for I know that you seek Jesus who was crucified. He is not here; for He is risen, as He said. Come, see the place where the Lord lay" (Matthew 28:5-6 NKJ).

Another angel spoke and said, "Why do you seek the living among the dead? He is not here, but is risen! . . ." (Luke 24:5-6 NKJ).

Finally, in the Book of Revelation, Jesus said, "I am He who lives, and was dead, and behold, I am alive forevermore. Amen. And I have the keys of Hades and of Death" (Revelation 1:18 NKJ).

The Great Physician

His Lordship over life and death naturally includes sickness and disease as well. He demonstrated this through His many healings.

One day a Roman soldier came to Jesus. His servant was sick and he wanted Jesus to heal him. Jesus said He would be glad to come to the soldier's house and heal his servant. But the Roman soldier, knowing that the Jews could not go to a Gentile house, said, "Lord, I'm not worthy to have you come under my roof. You just speak the word and my servant will be healed."

Now, this man as a Roman solider understood authority. He had a commander to whom he reported and had command over one hundred soldiers himself. So he said to Jesus, "I am a man under authority. I tell my men to go and they go. I tell them to come and they come. I tell my servant to do a certain thing and he does it."

The soldier recognized that Jesus also had authority. He realized that all Jesus had to do was to speak a word and his servant would be healed. Jesus was pleased with the man's faith and honored it by exercising His authority over the servant's sickness. The servant was instantly healed. (See Matthew 8:5-13.)

Because Jesus is Lord over death, sickness and disease, Christians will eventually experience victory over them as well. John put it this way in the Book of Revelation, "And God shall wipe away all tears from their eyes; and there shall be no more death, neither sorrow, nor crying, neither shall there be any more pain: for the former things are passed away" (Revelation 21:4 KJV).

Jesus—Lord Over The Spirit World

Jesus also proved that He is Lord over the *spirit world*. Mark recorded the following episode when Jesus was teaching in the synagogue. He wrote, "Then they went into Capernaum, and immediately on the Sabbath He entered the synagogue and taught. And they were astonished at His teaching, for He taught them as one having authority, and not as the scribes. Now there was a man in their synagogue with an unclean spirit. And he cried out, saying, 'Let us alone! What have we to do with You, Jesus of Nazareth? Have You come to destroy us? I know who You are—the Holy One of God!' But Jesus rebuked him, saying, 'Be quiet, and come out of him!' Then when the unclean spirit had convulsed him and cried out with a loud voice, he came out of him. Then they were all amazed, so that they questioned among themselves, saying, 'What is this? What new doctrine is this? For with authority, He commands even the unclean spirits, and they obey Him.' And immediately His fame spread throughout all the region around Galilee" (Mark 1:21-29 NKJ).

Trembling Spirits

One day Jesus met a man who was possessed by many demons. (See Mark 5:1-20.) He was a wild man who lived among the tombs. He didn't wear clothes. The townspeople had tried to bind up the man, but each time they tried, the demons in the man broke the chains. He would beat his body with stones and terrifyingly cry out night and day. No one could do anything with him.

But when Jesus met the man, the demons in the man recognized His authority over them. They begged Jesus not to send them into the bottomless pit. Now there was a herd of pigs on a nearby hill overlooking the Sea of Galilee. Jesus sent the demons into these pigs. When the demons

44

entered the pigs, they went crazy and stampeded over the side of the cliff into the sea.

8/29 *Dueteromy.*

Ruler Of The Unseen World

Peter preached "how God anointed Jesus of Nazareth with the Holy Spirit and with power, who went about doing good and healing all who were oppressed by the devil, for God was with Him" (Acts 10:38 NKJ).

Throughout His ministry, Jesus demonstrated that He had authority over Satan and demons. Paul said in Ephesians that Jesus is far above all principality, and power, and might, and dominion, and every name that is named, not only in this world but also in the world which is to come (1:21).

Peter spoke of Jesus, "who is gone into heaven, and is on the right hand of God; angels and authorities and powers been made subject unto him" (1 Peter 3:22 KJV).

The writer of Hebrews said that Jesus has destroyed (made powerless) him that had the power of death, that is, the devil (Hebrews 2:14).

In the Book of Revelation, Jesus has Satan bound for one-thousand years. This is during the physical rule of Jesus Christ on planet earth. At the end of the one thousand years Satan is set free. At that time, he makes one last desperate attempt to overthrow Jesus. But Jesus exercies His Lordship over Satan and casts him into hell (Revelation 20:10). *The spirit world must obey Him.*

Jesus—Lord Over Humanity

Jesus is Lord over all of *humanity*. It certainly does not seem that this is true. Much of the world has not even heard of Jesus, much less acknowledged that He is Lord. But one day the whole world will confess that He is Lord.

Paul expressed it this way, "Therefore God also has highly exalted Him and given Him the name which is above every name, that at the name of Jesus every knee should bow, of those in heaven, and of those on earth, and of those under the earth, and that every tongue should confess that Jesus

45

Christ is Lord, to the glory of God the Father" (Philippians 2:9-11 NKJ).

There are many passages in the Old Testament that speak about the universal Lordship of Jesus. Some of these are: Psalm 2; Isaiah 9:6-7; Daniel 2:31-45; Daniel 7; Zechariah 14:9, 16. These passages refer to the present universal Lordship of Jesus and His future rule on planet earth as King of kings and Lord of lords.

If you have never acknowledged Jesus Christ as your Lord, the Word of God to you is "that if you confess with your mouth the Lord Jesus and believe in your heart that God has raised Him from the dead, you will be saved. For with the heart one believes to righteousness, and with the mouth confession is made to salvation. For the Scripture says, *'Whoever believes on Him will not be put to shame.'* For there is no distinction between Jew and Greek, for the same Lord over all is rich to all who call upon Him. For *'whoever calls upon the name of the Lord shall be saved'* " (Romans 10:9-13 NKJ).

Whoever acknowledges Jesus Christ as their personal Lord will be saved from sin, saved from Satan and saved from death.

Jesus—Lord Over The Church

Finally, Jesus is Lord over the *Church.* Paul wrote to the Colossian Christians, "And he [Jesus] is the head of the body, the church: who is the beginning, the firstborn from the dead; that in all things he might have the preeminence" (Colossians 1:18 KJV).

Paul also wrote to the Ephesians that God ". . . hath put all things under his feet, and gave him to be the head over all things to the church" (Ephesians 1:22 KJV).

Jesus is the head of His Church. Now when we say this, we must be reminded that the Chruch is not a religious organization or denomination. *The Church is a company of people who have been placed into spiritual union with Jesus Christ.* Jesus is the head of this company of people and we make up His spiritual body on planet earth.

The Head And The Body

The head has two basic functions in relationship to the body. The first function is to *rule*. Our head houses our mind which is the master organ of our body. Our mind controls all of our bodily functions and feelings and makes all the decisions for the members of our body. So the head exercises absolute rule over the rest of the body. As long as the members of your body obey the head, your body will be in good working order.

The second basic function of the head is to *give life*. The head is the source of life to the rest of the body. Your body can live without certain members. For example, if you were to lose a hand or an arm, it would be difficult for you to do many things. You would be handicapped, but you would not be dead. You can go on living with one hand or one arm. But you cannot go on living without your head. The head gives life to the rest of the body. Your body has no life in itself but only that which it receives from your head.

This means that your head and your body have an organic relationship. The word "organic" refers to matter that has characteristics of life. The human body is an organism. We are living dynamic beings pulsating with life. Life flows continuously from our head to the individual members of our body through a system of nerves that connects the mind to the rest of our body. This nervous system serves as a dynamic communications network bringing life-giving messages from the mind to the rest of the body. However, if one of these nerves becomes pinched, this life-flow is hindered.

Divine Rule

In a similar way, Jesus is Lord over the Church. He is the ruler and source of life of every Christian. Paul stated that we are the purchased possessions of God (Ephesians 1:14). We are the purchased possessions of God the Father, paid for by God the Son and sealed by God the Holy Spirit.

Paul wrote to the Corinthians, "Haven't you yet learned that your body is the home of the Holy Spirit God gave you, and that he lives within you? Your own body does not belong to you. For God has bought you with a great price. So use every part of your body to give glory back to God, because he owns it" (1 Corinthians 6:19-20 TLB).

You see, God has a plan for your life. His overall plan for your life is that you live in His glory forever. This begins at the moment that you come to Christ as your Lord and Savior and receive the Holy Spirit. God then desires to live His very own life through your body while using you as an instrument for furthering His plans and purposes on planet earth.

So God has a specific plan for your life, and He desires that you learn this plan and give your life to executing it in loving trust and obedience. *He makes this plan known to you and gives you the power to execute it as you allow Jesus Christ to rule over you as your Lord and Master.* When you appropriate Jesus as your Lord, the Holy Spirit reveals to you the will of God for your life and then energizes you to be able to fulfill that will.

Paul expressed it this way to the Romans: "I beseech you therefore, brethren, by the mercies of God, that you present your bodies a living sacrifice, holy, acceptable to God, which is your reasonable service. And do not be conformed to this world, but be transformed by the renewing of your mind, that you may prove what is that good and acceptable and perfect will of God" (Romans 12:1-2 NKJ).

Divine Life

Just as the head is the source of life to the body, Jesus is the source of the God-kind of life in the Spirit. When we appropriate Him as our Lord, the Holy Spirit takes over our life and lives the life of Jesus Christ through us. We become living, dynamic beings pulsating with the very life of God. *The God-kind of life flows continuously through us by the Holy Spirit Who operates as a divine nervous system bringing this life from Jesus our head to us.*

We are a company of people who receive life from another person. This is what Paul meant when he wrote that

48

"Christ . . . is our life" (Colossians 3:4). *The only thing that will stop this life from flowing is if we "pinch a spiritual nerve" by grieving the Holy Spirit.*

This is why Paul wrote to the Philippians, "Therefore, my beloved, as you have always obeyed, not as in my presence only, but now much more in my absence, work out your own salvation with fear and trembling; for it is God who works in you both to will and to do for His good pleasure" (Philippians 2:12-13 NKJ).

Appropriating His Lordship

Dear reader, you cannot make Jesus Lord. He already is Lord. Jesus Christ is the Lord of the universe Who has become our Savior. But you can appropriate His Lordship in your own personal life. In fact, you must do this in order to live the victorious Christian life.

Paul said it this way to the Romans, "We are not our own bosses to live or die as we ourselves might choose. Living or dying we follow the Lord. Either way we are his. Christ died and rose again for this very purpose, so that he can be our Lord both while we live and when we die" (Romans 14:7-9 TLB).

Perhaps you know Jesus as your personal Savior, but you have never invited Him to rule in every area of your life. I pray that you will do so right now as this is God's will for you. You do this by recognizing His claim on your life and presenting yourself to Him in loving trust and obedience. As you do, Jesus will continuously share His God-kind of life with you through the Holy Spirit.

Chapter 4—Appropriating His Lordship

Review Exercise 3

1. Give your definition of the word "Lord."

2. How did Jesus prove His Lordship?

3. List five aspects of Jesus' Lordship.

    a.

    b.

    c.

    d.

    e.

4. How can you apply this knowledge to your life?

5
Walking In The Spirit

We've now examined two of the three steps we must take in order to live the victorious Christian life. These are to realize your identification with Christ and to appropriate Him as Lord of your life. You are now ready to take the third step which is to "walk in the Spirit." *Walking in the Spirit simply means allowing the Holy Spirit of God Who is in you to live the life of Christ out of you.*

Walking In The Spirit

Paul wrote about this third step of faith to the Christians in Galatia. He said, "I say then: Walk in the Spirit, and you shall not fulfill the lust of the flesh. For the flesh lusts against the Spirit, and the Spirit against the flesh; and these are contrary to one another, so that you do not do the things that you wish. But if you are led by the Spirit, you are not under the law" (Galatians 5:16-18 NKJ).

These Christians in Galatia were desiring to live the abundant Christian life, but they were failing miserably. The reason they were failing is *they were attempting to live this victorious Christian life by trying to keep a lot of rules and regulations and do's and don'ts.* And the harder they tried, the more they failed. The more New Year's resolutions they made, the more they broke. As soon as they got off their knees promising God that they "would never do it again," they did it again. (Sound familiar?)

You see, they did not understand that it was Jesus Himself who would live this life through them. They thought they had to live it for Him. But the harder they tried the more they failed. They soon discovered that they did not have the power within themselves to live this victorious Christian life. And the do's and don'ts even made their failures more obvious. There soon developed a big credibility gap between what Jesus promised and what they were experiencing. Doesn't this sound familiar? So Paul wrote this letter to these Christians to instruct them (and us) on how to live the victorious Christian life. His instruction is to "Walk in the Spirit and you shall not fulfill the lust of the flesh."

The Inside War

Now you and I are different people (personalities). I cannot live your life and you cannot live mine. But if somehow I could get inside your body, I could live my life through you. My soul or personality, which is my mind, emotions and will, could be lived out through you. You would be walking in me and I in you. The two of us would become one in a beautiful union of our souls. The potential joys of such a relationship are beyond human comprehension.

But suppose that once I'm inside you, you decide that you don't want me to live my life through you. You decide that you want to live your own life. If you make that decision, you and I are going to be warring with each other to see whose life is going to be lived through you. The result is that you will be miserable and I will be grieved.

Now this is impossible between two human beings. Our souls are bound to our bodies as long as our bodies are alive. We are always going to be separated because we are physical beings. I cannot get inside you and you cannot get inside me. Our souls may be in unison, but we're still going to be separated by our physical bodies.

But this is not true with God. God is Spirit (John 4:24). He is a personal Spirit with a mind, emotions and a will. God is not an "it." He is a Spirit with personality and character. And since a spirit is not bound to a physical body, a spirit can get inside a human being.

A Jesus Invasion

God's Spirit is called the Holy Spirit (John 20:22). The Holy Spirit is everywhere; therefore, He can get inside (inhabit) any and all persons who will invite Him into their life. The Holy Spirit will then live the very life of Jesus Christ through the person who receives Him. This is what it means to walk in the Spirit. You simply allow the Holy Spirit to rule over your soul and live the life of Christ in you. As I mentioned in Chapter One, you don't actually live this life yourself, but you live "in it."

Since Jesus has a human body, He cannot get inside you, but the Holy Spirit can. So when you ask Jesus to come into your life, He actually sends you the Holy Spirit. Jesus spoke of this as being born again, or born from above (John 3:1-8). *Jesus lives His life and personality (mind, emotions and will) through you by the Holy Spirit.* (See Philippians 2:13.)

Look up.

You and Jesus have become one in a beautiful union of your spirit with the Holy Spirit Who seals you in the Christ. (See Ephesians 1:13, 4:30; 2 Corinthians 1:22).

The Divine Seal

In ancient times, the king would place his seal or marking on a document to identify it with him and establish its legitimacy and credibility. The king's seal would actually become part of the document. This would be much like a

53

person's birth certificate containing the seal of the state that issued the certificate. The state seal is actually part of the certificate.

In a similar way, *the Holy Spirit is the divine seal of God joining you to Himself.* But suppose that, once the Holy Spirit is inside you, you then decide that you do not want Him to live the life of Christ through you. You decide that you are not going to allow the Holy Spirit to rule over your soul. Well, guess what is going to happen? Your old Adam-like nature and the Holy Spirit will war with each other to see whose life is going to be controlling you and lived through you. *You are going to be miserable and the Holy Spirit will be grieved.* Paul had this in mind when he wrote to the Ephesians, "And do not grieve the Holy Spirit of God, by whom you were sealed for [unto] the day of redemption [of your body]" (4:30 NKJ).

The Battle For You

This is the war that goes on inside every Christian. Paul described it so well in Galatians 5:17 referenced above, "For the flesh [Adam-like nature] lusts against the Spirit, and the Spirit against the flesh; and these are contrary to one another, so that you do not do the things that you wish." The result is a "spiritual heartburn." You are not enjoying Jesus and you can't enjoy sin. You are the most miserable of all creatures.

A lot of Christians don't understand this internal "tug of war." They are not aware that this is taking place within them. So when they begin to experience it, they don't know what their problem is or how to deal with it. They either think that God has left them, the Bible is not really true or that there is something dreadfully wrong with them. Many just despair over the situation and settle for a defeated life.

The Works Of The Flesh

Now if you are unaware of this internal war, it is easy for the old Adam-like nature (the old man) to regain power

54

over you. When the old man regains power, you are going to sin. Paul spoke of this sin as the *"works of the flesh."*

He wrote, "Now the works of the flesh are evident, which are: adultery, fornication, uncleanness, licentiousness, idolatry, sorcery, hatred, contentions, jealousies, outbursts of wrath, selfish ambitions, dissensions, heresies, envy, murders, drunkenness, revelries, and the like; of which I tell you beforehand, just as I also told you in time past, that those who practice such things will not inherit the kingdom of God" (Galatians 5:19-21 NKJ).

In the Bible, the word "flesh" is often used to speak of our old Adam-like nature—our old man. This is the way Paul used it in this passage. *So the works of the flesh are the sins we commit while being dominated by the old man.* It is our sinful nature manifesting itself through our body.

A New Lifestyle

Paul said that people who practice (continually keep on doing) works of the flesh will not inherit the kingdom of God. Now by this, he didn't mean that once you become a Christian you will never sin again. Christians aren't perfect, they are forgiven. He meant you will not continue living in sin. The desires of your heart and your life style, which was characterized by sin before you became a Christian, will change.

You can't keep on continually living in the works of the flesh. There will be a change in your life. *If there is no change in your life, then it demonstrates that you have never been to the cross of Jesus Christ and crucified your old Adam-like nature with Him.* You have never gotten out of Adam and into Christ. Therefore, you cannot inherit the kingdom of God.

Jesus said it this way in Matthew 12:33: ". . . a tree is known by its fruit" (NKJ). He earlier said, "Beware of false prophets, who come to you in sheep's clothing, but inwardly they are ravenous wolves. You will know them by their fruits. Do men gather grapes from thornbushes or figs from thistles? Even so, every good tree bears good fruit, but a bad

55

tree bears bad fruit. A good tree cannot bear bad fruit, nor can a bad tree bear good fruit. Every tree that does not bear good fruit is cut down and thrown into the fire. Therefore by their fruits you will know them" (Matthew 7:15-20 NKJ).

Jesus then went on to say, "Not all who sound religious are really godly people. They may refer to me as 'Lord,' but still won't get to heaven. For the decisive question is whether they obey my Father in heaven. At the Judgment many will tell me, 'Lord, Lord, we told others about you and used your name to cast out demons and to do many other great miracles.' But I will reply, 'You have never been mine. Go away, for your deeds are evil" (Matthew 7:21-23 TLB).

Perhaps God is speaking to your heart about this matter. Maybe you have always thought you were a Christian but there has never been a change in your life. I must tell you with the greatest of tenderness and love that you are not a Christian. But you can be a Christian by turning from your sins and asking Christ to come into your life. If you have never done this, please stop reading and do so now.

Being Cultivated

One of the things I've noticed about fruit is that it does not grow overnight. Once the seed is planted in the ground, the ground must then be cultivated. There must be sun and water and fertilization. The weeds must be pulled so as not to smother the seed.

The planter gives a lot of tender love and care to that seed. He checks on it regularly. Finally his care is rewarded when he sees that seed pushing up through the ground as a green blade full of promise. That little green blade grows into a firm stalk. The stalk wonderously produces buds that gloriously blossom into delicious fruit. But this all takes time and attention.

In John 15, Jesus made a spiritual comparison to this process. He said that God is the farmer and we are His field (John 15:1-7). God plants the seed of the Holy Spirit in us the moment we come to Christ. Then God begins to cultivate us so that over a period of time that seed of the Holy Spirit will produce fruit in us. *And with what does God cultivate us? He cultivates us with His Word, the Holy Scriptures.* We learn from Psalm 1, "Blessed is the man that walketh not in the counsel of the ungodly, nor standeth in the way of sinners, nor sitteth in the seat of the scornful. But his delight is in the law of the Lord; and in his law doth he meditate day and night. And he shall be like a tree planted by the rivers of water, that bringeth forth his fruit in his season; his leaf also shall not wither; and whatsoever he doeth shall prosper" (vv. 1-3 KJV).

God cultivates us as we meditate on His Word. To meditate means to give your thoughts in careful attention and study. It is more than just a casual reading. Jesus said we are made clean through His Word (John 15:3). David wrote in Psalm 119:11, "Thy word have I hid in mine heart, that I might not sin against thee' (KJV).

God's Human Field

If you are a Christian, God's seed of the Holy Spirit has been planted in your heart. That's where the cultivation takes place, in your heart, not in your head. But it requires meditation for God's Word to get into your heart. *As you meditate on God's Word, the Holy Spirit will take His words off the pages of the Bible and root them in your heart.* In this way, the Word of God will begin to form and grow in you and become part of your very being. As this cultivation takes place, God uses His Word to weed out the works of the flesh so that the fruit of the Spirit can come forth.

This means that you must have a consistent time of daily meditation on God's Word. There is simply no other way for God to cultivate you. There are no short-cuts. Many Christians are like withering leaves because they do not take the time to be cultivated. *You must make a commitment to discipline yourself to meditate daily on God's Word.* May I suggest you mark off forty-five minutes each day on your calendar and call it "cultivation time." Stick with it for at least six weeks until it becomes a habit for you. I can assure you that as God's Word begins to grow in you the fruit of His Spirit will come forth.

The Fruit Of The Spirit

Let's now consider the *fruit of the Spirit*. Paul mentioned it also in his letter to the Galatians. Here's what he said: ". . . the fruit of the Spirit is love, joy, peace, longsuffering, gentleness [kindness], goodness, faith [faithfulness], meekness, temperance [self-control]: against such there is no law" (Galatians 5:22-23 KJV).

Notice that this is the fruit of the Spirit. It is not our fruit. The Holy Spirit is the One who lives the life of Christ in us. We don't live it ourselves. Instead, we live in it. *The fruit of the Spirit is the character and life of Jesus Christ being lived out of us by the Holy Spirit.* We don't get this character from God; we get God Who is this character. This is God's very own life coming to live in us through the Holy Spirit. Since it's His life we receive, rather than things we get, Paul spoke of it in the singular as the fruit (not fruits) of the Spirit.

This is the abundant life Jesus was speaking about in John 10:10. It is the eternal life of God breathed into us so that we might live forever with Him. And when this God-kind of life controls us, we find fulfillment, contentment and freedom from the fear of want and death. *As the Holy Spirit lives this life out of us, we walk in authority, power and victory over sin, Satan and eventually death itself.*

So you see, Jesus wasn't talking about Cadillacs, fur coats and diamond rings. Now there is nothing wrong with having these things. God does desire that we prosper, but not at the expense of our soul. John wrote, "Beloved, I pray that you may prosper in all things and be in health, just as your soul prospers" (3 John 2 NKJ). *The fruit of the Spirit is prosperity of the soul. It is the life of Jesus Christ growing in us as the Holy Spirit applies God's Word to our hearts.* Let's now briefly examine this portrait of Jesus Christ.

Love

The first fruit that Paul mentioned is love. *God's love is different from human love in that God's love is uncaused.* When we love someone it's because we find something that we believe is lovable in the one we love. The person becomes the object of our love.

Human Love

There are two kinds of human love that can be called forth from us. *These are physical love and soulish love.* Because of our fallen nature, human love is usually first manifested at the physical level. For example, our first impressions of people are normally based on what they look like. People naturally don't enjoy being around others whose appearance is unpleasant to them. So, as we all know, physical love pertains to the body. The Greeks used the word "eros" to refer to physical love.

The second manifestation of human love is at the soulish level. We often think of our soul in terms of our personality. Our personality expresses our individual uniqueness; it's what makes us different. And we all have different personalities. Even though we all have a need for fellowship, we don't like to be around people whom we perceive to have an unpleasant personality. So we see there is something we believe to be lovable about another person's soul that calls forth our soulish love so that we desire fellowship with certain people. The Greeks used the word "phileo" to refer to this soulish kind of love. Both "eros" and "phileo" are awakened and aroused by something we perceive to be lovable in another person. *Therefore, human love is a caused love called forth by an external object.*

God's Love

God's love is different from human love in that it is uncaused. God does not love out of passion or emotion. God loves because love is Who God is in His being. It is His nature to love. *This means that God's love has nothing to do with the object of His love.* It is not a "called out" love based on the lovableness of an external object. God loves the unlovable as well as the lovable because God is love (1 John 4:7-8). In fact, in God's eyes, all of us are unlovable because we have all sinned and come short of His glory.

There is no reason for God's love towards us except Himself. This is a love for the spirit of a person. It is an uncaused, unconditional love. This kind of love was unknown to man so the Greeks had to make up a brand-new word to describe it. They called it "agape" love. This is God's kind of love that is freely given without any consideration of the lovableness or merit of its object.

Now isn't this just the kind of love we all need? It sure is. But how can we have this kind of love? Paul told us in his letter to the Romans, ". . . the love of God has been poured out in our hearts by the Holy Spirit who was given to us" (Romans 5:5 NKJ).

You see, we receive God's love into our hearts when we receive God Himself into our hearts. It's not so much that we get love, but we get God Who is love. *As we walk in the Spirit, God's unconditional love flows out of us.* We find that we are able to love others regardless of who or what they are. The one who is "love Himself" loves through you. You can't help but love. You may weep. Your heart may break. But you will love. *So you see, you don't really need to pray for more of God's love. You just need to surrender to that love God has already placed in you by the Holy Spirit.*

This agape love is the true test of our relationship with Jesus Christ. Jesus said it this way, "A new commandment I give to you, that you love one another; as I have loved you, that you also love one another. By this all will know that you are My disciples, if you have love for one another" (John 13:34-35 NKJ).

Joy

The next fruit Paul mentioned is joy. Joy is not the same thing as happiness. Happiness is a fleeting feeling based on external circumstances. If things are going well for you,

you are happy. If things are not going well for you, you are sad. People's lives are like a thermometer; they feel up and down based on external circumstances. When we're not happy, we wallow in self-pity. We get easily discouraged and depressed. We murmer and complain. We question God's sovereignty and that He is working all things for our good. We let circumstances dictate our feelings and control our state of mind.

Joy is different. *Joy is an internal, eternal delight in God.* It is not tied to circumstances. You can be satisfied and content regardless of what is going on around you when you have joy.

God is our source of joy. He is perfectly content with Himself. The Prophet Nehemiah recognized this and wrote, ". . . for the joy of the LORD is your strength" (Nehemiah 8:10 KJV).

Isaiah said that when the Messiah came, He would give us this joy. For those who mourn, the Messiah would ". . . give unto them beauty for ashes, the oil of joy for mourning, the garment of praise for the spirit of heaviness; that they might be called trees of righteousness, the planting of the LORD, that he might be glorified" (Isaiah 61:3 KJV).

God gives us His joy when we come to Jesus Christ. Paul wrote, ". . . but we also joy in God through our Lord Jesus Christ . . ." (Romans 5:11 KJV). This is true because we can know God through Jesus Christ. And when we come to know God we find the One Who Himself is joy. Our delight is in Him, not in our circumstances.

Jesus said He would put this eternal joy of God in us and that it would be there permanently (John 15:11; 16:22-24). *This joy becomes real to us when we are controlled by the Holy Spirit Who is our joy.* This is what Paul meant when he wrote, "for the kingdom of God is not food and drink, but righteousness and peace and joy in the Holy Spirit" (Romans 14:17 NKJ).

David wrote that fullness of joy comes by being in the presence of God (Psalm 16:11). We are in the direct presence of God when we are controlled by the Holy Spirit. *If your life is like a thermometer, up one day and down the next, you can find joy in God.*

The Prophet Habakkuk learned this key to divine happiness and wrote, "Although the fig tree shall not blossom, neither shall fruit be in the vines; the labour of the olive shall fail, and the fields shall yield no meat; the flock shall be cut off from the fold, and there shall be no herd in the stalls: Yet I will rejoice in the LORD, I will joy in the God of my salvation" (Habakkuk 3:17-18 KJV).

Peace

Peace is a calmness and rest in a person's soul. It too comes from God Who is called the God of all peace (Romans 15:33). This peace is available to us through Jesus Whom the Bible speaks of as the "prince of peace" (Isaiah 9:6). When Jesus was born the angels proclaimed, "Glory to God in the highest, and on earth peace, good will toward men" (Luke 2:14 NKJ).

In the last chapter we looked in on a raging storm that came upon the Sea of Galilee. The boat Jesus and His disciples were in was tossed to and fro by the waves of the storm. The disciples were afraid. But Jesus slept peacefully in spite of the storm.

We have many raging storms in our life. The waves of these storms of life toss us to and fro. We become anxious. We are afraid we might sink in the seas of distress and worry and fear. *We all desperately need the peace of God.*

Jesus gives this peace to all who will come to Him. He told His disciples, "Peace I leave with you, My peace I give to you; not as the world gives do I give to you. Let not your heart be troubled, neither let it be afraid. . . . These things I have spoken to you, that in Me you may have peace. In the world you will have tribulation; but be of good cheer, I have overcome the world" (John 14:27; 16:33 NKJ).

Paul wrote to the Philippians, "Be anxious for nothing, but in everything by prayer and supplication, with thanksgiving, let your requests be made known to God;

and the peace of God, which surpasses all understanding, will guard your hearts and minds through Christ Jesus" (Philippians 4:6-7 NKJ).

Paul likened the peace of God to a guard who keeps away the enemy. The enemy in this case is worry, doubt, fear, anxiety, etc. *The peace of God will guard both your heart and mind so that you can have rest in your soul in the midst of the stormy seas of life.*

The Prophet Isaiah gave us the formula for peace. He said, "He [God] will keep in perfect peace all those who trust in him, whose thoughts turn often to the Lord! Trust in the Lord God always, for in the Lord Jehovah is your ever-lasting strength" (Isaiah 26:3-4 TLB).

Isaiah went on to say that there is no peace for the wicked. They are like the stormy sea, always churning, always restless, always troubled (Isaiah 57:20-21). But we have peace with God through the blood of Jesus Christ and the peace of God by walking in the Spirit.

Longsuffering

Longsuffering is steadfast patience and endurance that enables us to persevere in spite of difficult circumstances and difficult people.

It doesn't take us long to realize that life is not always a bed of roses. We have to do things we don't particularly like. We spend much of our life waiting for things to happen. We have difficult trials. People rub us the wrong way.

Without God, people can't endure the hardships of life. They fall apart with the least bit of pressure. The least little ailment, resistance or difficulty makes them give up. They run from their difficulty. They act in haste. They do something foolish for which they are later sorry. They speak a quick word of anger. They can't endure.

God is our source of longsuffering. Psalm 86:15 tells us, "But thou, O Lord, art a God full of compassion, and gracious, longsuffering, and plenteous in mercy and truth" (KJV). Moses wrote, "The LORD is longsuffering . . ." (Numbers 14:18 KJV). Peter declared, "The Lord is not slack concerning His promise, as some count slackness, but is longsuffering toward us, not willing that any should perish but that all should come to repentance" (2 Peter 3:9 NKJ).

Jesus showed us God's longsuffering. His trials were a mockery. The physical beating He endured was beyond belief. First they stripped Him naked and laid thirty-nine cruel lashes on Him that tore chunks of flesh out of His back. They spit in His face, pulled the hair out of His head, struck Him with their open hand and then again with their fist. They hit Him on the head with a club and beat Him so badly that He was hardly recognizable as a human being. They pressed a crown of thorns on His head and mocked Him. Then they took Him and crucified Him. They did all of this even though the Roman governor said he could find no fault in Him. Yet in spite of this greatest of all injustices, the Bible says that Jesus opened not His mouth (Matthew 27:14). He endured to the end.

Immediately we recognize our need for this God-given ability to endure. We need help "hanging in there" with difficult circumstances and difficult people. We need a divine strength and toughness that will enable us to "keep on keeping on." Jesus said those who endure to the end will be saved (Matthew 24:13). Paul endured all things for the sake of the elect (2 Timothy 2:10). We are encouraged to endure and be steadfast (2 Timothy 2:12). *The Holy Spirit works this longsuffering in us enabling us to persevere through difficult trials and tribulation. Walk in the Spirit and you will find a supernatural courage and ability that will sustain you through any hardship.*

Paul's words of encouragement to the Corinthians are appropriate for us today. He wrote, "Therefore, my beloved brethren, be steadfast, immovable, always abounding in the work of the Lord, knowing that your labor is not in vain in the Lord" (1 Corinthians 15:58 NKJ).

Gentleness (kindness)

Gentleness (some translations read kindness) may be thought of as *warmhearted tenderness*. If there's one thing the world needs, it's warmhearted tenderness. Unfortunately, people don't naturally have this characteristic. People can be very rude, rough and uncaring. They are like unbroken horses that don't care how rough your ride through life is or how many bumps and bruises you may have accumulated. We so need people to be gentle and kind towards us and they need us to be gentle and kind toward them. But so often do we disappoint and hurt each other.

Only God is able to show the warmhearted tenderness we all long for and need. Isaiah likened God's gentleness to a shepherd who tenderly cares for his flock. He wrote of God, "He shall feed his flock like a shepherd: he shall gather the lambs with his arm, and carry them in his bosom, and shall gently lead those that are with young" (Isaiah 40:11 KJV).

Nehemiah spoke of his people's rebellion against God but took comfort in God's kindness. He said ". . . but thou art a God ready to pardon, gracious and merciful, slow to anger, and of great kindness . . ." (Nehemiah 9:17 KJV).

Jonah learned about God's kindness when God had mercy on the people of Nineveh. He said, ". . . for I knew that thou art a gracious God, and merciful, slow to anger and of great kindness . . ." (Jonah 4:2 KJV).

We see this same gentle kindness in Jesus Christ. Little children felt at ease with Jesus. When they crowded around Him, He would pick them up, sit them on His lap and tenderly hold them in His strong arms and rough carpenters' hands. Both the rich and the poor would approach Him. Men and women felt comfortable around Him, Jew, Gentiles and Samaritans were touched by the warmth of His tender compassion. People felt safe with Jesus. They could be themselves. They could pour out their heart to Him. He understood human frailties. He was gentle and kind, like a cool breeze on a hot summer day.

Don't you wish more people would be gentle and kind to you? Perhaps they would if you were more gentle and kind to them. And you can be because Jesus has put this quality within you by the Holy Spirit.

65

Paul wrote to the Ephesians, "Let all bitterness, wrath, anger, clamor, and evil speaking be put away from you, with all malice. And be kind to one another, tenderhearted, forgiving one another, just as God in Christ also forgave you" (Ephesians 4:31-32 NKJ).

He reminded the Thessalonians of his own example of gentleness when he ministered among them. He recalled to their minds that ". . . we were as gentle among you as a mother feeding and caring for her own children" (1 Thessalonians 2:7 TLB)

When you are gentle and kind, people will feel easy around you. They will not be afraid to come to you with their burdens. They will open their hearts to you. They will share their bumps and bruises with you. Your warmhearted tenderness will help make their ride through life a lot easier. *As you walk in the Spirit, you will be able to do unto others as you would have them do unto you.*

Goodness

Goodness is a desire to bless others with lovingkindness and goodwill. Now we humans don't naturally spend our time determining how we can bless others. We spend our time thinking about ourselves. We are not warm goodhearted creatures with only a few little wrinkles that need to be ironed out. Anyone who thinks that man is basically good hasn't read the papers in a long, long time. But wouldn't the world be a much better place to live if people were good to each other? Don't you wish people were good to you? I bet people wish you were good to them.

But only God is naturally good (Matthew 19:17). Goodness is who God is in His very essence and being. God doesn't *try* to be good; He *is* good. All that flows out of God is good. Every good and perfect gift comes from Him Who moves the course of world events for the good of those who love Him and have been called according to His purpose. (See Romans 8:28; James 1:17.) After thinking about all that God had done for him, the Psalmist wrote, ". . . O give thanks unto the Lord; for he is good . . ." (Psalm 106:1 KJV).

Now we are very moody creatures. Our dispositions are constantly changing. We are never sure just how to approach people because we don't know what kind of mood they are in. We don't know if they are going to be in a good mood or a bad mood. But we don't have this problem with God. *God is always in a good mood.* We read in Psalm 52:1, ". . . the goodness of God endureth continually" (KJV). We can approach God knowing that we will always find Him in a good mood.

We see God's goodness perfectly revealed in Jesus Christ. It was said of Jesus in Acts 10:38 that, "He went about doing good." Well, of course He did. He was goodness in the flesh. Jesus was good by nature; everything flowing out of Him was good. He was the perfect revelation of God's steadfast lovingkindness and goodwill toward His creatures.

God desires to bless us with His lovingkindness and goodwill. We receive this goodness of God when we come to Christ. God then desires to reveal His goodness through us to others. He wants us, by the Holy Spirit, to be channels of His goodness.

Jesus said to all His followers, "Let your light so shine before men, that they may see your good works, and glorify your Father which is in heaven" (Matthew 5:16 KJV).

John wrote, "Beloved, do not imitate what is evil, but what is good. He who does good is of God, but he who does evil has not seen God" (3 John 11 NKJ).

People will see the light of God's goodness in you when you walk in the Spirit. You will be a blessing to those around you as the warm rays of His light shine on them.

Faith (Faithfulness)

The next fruit to be cultivated is faith or faithfulness. *Faithfulness is a steadfast commitment.* You know it's hard to get people to make a commitment. They say they will do something but they don't do it. They say they will be somewhere, but they don't show up. People just aren't dependable. You can't rely on them. They don't keep their promises. They will disappoint you. They are not faithful.

Maybe they will, maybe they won't; you never know what they are going to do.

But God is faithful. You can depend on Him. Moses wrote, "Know therefore that the LORD thy God, he is God, the faithful God, which keepeth covenant and mercy with them that love him and keep his commandments to a thousand generations" (Deuteronomy 7:9 KJV).

God is a covenant-keeping God. He is faithful to keep His covenants. He is faithful to keep His Word. He keeps His commitments and promises. If God says that He will do something, then He will do it. If God says He will be somewhere, then He'll be there.

God is faithful to save all who will call upon Him. He is faithful to keep us from failing and to present us before His presence with exceeding joy. He is faithful not to give us any trial too difficult for us to handle by His grace.

We can depend on God. We can trust Him. God is reliable. He won't disappoint you. He is steadfastly committed to all that He is, all that He says and all that He does.

God promised to come to the earth and give His own life as the innocent substitutionary sacrifice for the forgiveness of our sins. He kept this promise in Jesus Christ. Jesus was born exactly as God promised. Jesus was faithful to give us the Word of God. He was faithful to do the works of God. He was faithful unto death. God was faithful to raise Jesus from the dead and sit Him on the throne of the universe. Jesus was faithful to send the Holy Spirit as He promised He would. In Revelation 1:5, Jesus is called the faithful witness.

Now we are to be faithful. Jesus said, "Be faithful until death, and I will give you the crown of life" (Revelation 2:10 NKJ). *As we walk in the Spirit, we can be faithful.* We can be faithful to God and faithful to each other. We can be dependable, loyal, reliable and trustworthy. When we say we are going to do something, we will be able to do it. When we say we are going to be somewhere, we'll be there.

We can be faithful to our word. We'll keep our promises and our commitments. We'll be faithful in our work, faithful in our studies, faithful in our worship, faithful in our giving and faithful in our relationships. We will be faithful and steadfastly committed to all we say and do because God is faithful.

Meekness

Meekness is allowing God to deal with you without disputing His dealings. The person who is meek does not have an inflated view of his importance. He has no ego or pride. He's submissive and receives instruction. He has a teachable spirit.

We don't like the word "meek." This is because we don't really understand it's meaning. When we hear the word "meek," we think of someone who is weak. Our minds picture some mousy little person who sits in the corner and never opens his mouth. But this is not the biblical meaning of the word. *Meekness is power.* It is the power to allow God or anyone else to deal justly with you without defending ourselves. Any weakling can strike back. It doesn't take much strength to argue and demand your rights. Anybody can murmur and complain. The real strong are those who are meek.

The two bravest men who ever walked the face of the earth were Moses and Jesus. Moses dared to confront Pharaoh with the demand to "Let my people go." He led the Hebrews out of Egypt. He was used by God to part the Red Sea. He stood in the presence of God and received the Ten Commandments. He led the Hebrews for forty years and kept the nation together. What a powerful leader. Yet the Bible tells us that Moses was the meekest man on the face of the earth (Numbers 12:3).

The big, strong, tough, boisterous fishermen were frightened by the storm. Jesus slept through it. He confronted demons. He drove out the money changers. He healed the sick and raised the dead. He made bold claims about Himself. Yet Jesus was meek (Matthew 11:29). He said, "Blessed are the meek: for they shall inherit the earth" (Matthew 5:5 KJV).

God desires to work this same meekness in us by the Holy Spirit. He wants to empty us of our ego and pride. He wants us to be submissive. He wants us to receive instruction without murmuring and complaining. God wants us to recognize that we live and move and have our being in Him. He is the potter; we are the clay. He is the vine and we are the branches; without Him we can do nothing.

The Apostle James exhorted us to receive God's Word with meekness (James 1:21). Paul wrote to the Galatian Christians to restore those living in sin in a spirit of meekness (Galatians 6:1). He wrote to the Ephesians to walk, "With all lowliness and meekness, with longsuffering, forbearing one another in love" (Ephesians 4:2 KJV). To the Colossians he said, "Therefore, as the elect of God, holy and beloved, put on tender mercies, kindness, humbleness of mind, meekness, longsuffering; bearing with one another, and forgiving one another, if anyone has a complaint against another; even as Christ forgave you, so you also must do" (Colossians 3:12-13 NKJ).

Temperance, (Self-Control)

The last fruit is self-control. This is a quality we all so badly need. But we just don't have it within ourselves. We can't control our tongues, so we speak harsh words for which we are later sorry. We can't control our appetites (sorry about that) so we eat and drink more than we know we should. We can't control our minds so we think evil thoughts. We are not able to keep firm control on our passions, emotions and will. We grit our teeth and try with great self-effort and determination, but we fail. It seems hopeless at times, doesn't it?

Only God can bring self-control into our lives. God always works in a way consistent with His being. He never acts in a way that violates His character. He doesn't act out of passion or emotion. God is always in control. God has a plan and He moves the course of world history within that plan. He is the sovereign God Who is actively exercising absolute rule over His creation. God knows Who He is, and

He knows what He is doing. He is in control of Himself and He is in control of what He is doing.

Jesus perfectly revealed the self-control of God. He said He didn't come to do His own will but the will of His heavenly Father (John 5:30). He claimed that the words He spoke were not His own, but the Father's. He said the works He did and miracles He performed were done by the Father. Therefore, He told His followers, "He who has seen me has seen the Father" (John 14:9 NKJ).

Jesus was in control of every situation. Several times the authorities tried to arrest Jesus, but they couldn't. It wasn't because He defended Himself. It was because He was in control. If you'll carefully read the accounts of Jesus' arrest and trials, you will find that He was in control of the entire situation. They didn't arrest Him until He was ready to be arrested. They didn't try Him, beat Him and crucify Him until He was ready for them to do so. He was God in the flesh in control of everything He said, everything He did and all the people and circumstances surrounding Him.

God has made this same control available to us when we come to Christ. It's not us trying to control ourself by will power and determination. *It is the Holy Spirit living the self-controlled life of Jesus in us, through us and out of us.* Only when we come under His control do we have self-control. The Holy Spirit renews our minds, bridles our emotions and brings our will into obedience to God. The result is a divine discipline of our body, soul and spirit.

An Abundant Life

This is the abundant life Jesus came to give us. It's His very own God-kind of life in the Spirit. And what a life it is! It's just the kind of life we all yearn for and so desperately need. It's the "zoe" life. It's eternal life. It's abundant life. It's a fulfilled, contented life. It's love, joy, peace, longsuffering, gentleness, goodness, faithfulness, meekness, and temperance. *It's life in the Spirit.* It's ours when we realize our identification with Christ, appropriate His Lordship and walk in the Spirit.

Paul's concluding words on this subject to the Galatian Christians are appropriate for closing out this chapter. He said, "And they that are Christ's have crucified the flesh with the affections and lusts. If we live in the Spirit, let us also walk in the Spirit" (Galatians 5:24-25 KJV).

Review Exercise 4

1. Explain the internal tug of war that takes place within a Christian.

2. Explain what is meant by the phrase "works of the flesh."

3. Explain what is meant by the phrase "fruit of the Spirit."

4. How can you apply this knowledge to your life?

6
Ministering In The Spirit

The greatest news in the whole world is that God has taken the initiative to bring us into a covenant relationship with Himself through the blood of Jesus Christ. When we accept this covenant, we find forgiveness of sin and become partakers of the very life of God. As this God-kind of life controls us we have authority and power over sin, Satan and eventually death itself.

In these last chapters, we've learned how to enjoy the full blessings of this covenant relationship with God. We've discussed the three steps of identifying with Christ, appropriating His Lordship and walking in the Spirit. We now want to discover how to share this exciting life in the Spirit with others. We want to learn how to minister in the Spirit.

Being Filled With The Spirit

The key to ministering in the Spirit is to be filled with the Spirit. Paul wrote to the Ephesian Christians, ". . . be not drunk with wine, wherein is excess; but be filled with the Spirit" (Ephesians 5:18 KJV). Paul compared a Christian who is filled with the Holy Spirit to a person who is drunk with wine. The person who is drunk with wine is controlled by the wine. The person who is filled with the Holy Spirit is controlled by the Holy Spirit.

The purpose of being filled with the Holy Spirit is to release the power of God that is already within you, if you are a Christian. Jesus said it in these words, ". . . you shall receive power when the Holy Spirit has come upon you; and you will be witnesses to Me in Jerusalem, and in all Judea and Samaria, and to the end of the earth" (Acts 1:8 NKJ).

Sealed But Not Filled

As we've already learned, when people ask Christ to come into their life, Jesus sends them the Holy Spirit. The Holy Spirit comes to live in them and establishes their new life position in Christ. *So every Christian has the Holy Spirit.* Christians wouldn't be Christians if they didn't, because Christians are people who possess Christ in them through the person of the Holy Spirit (Romans 8:9).

However, it's painfully obvious that not every Christian lives in the Spirit and power of God. Not every Christian is walking in the dominion and authority of Jesus Christ in them. Not every Christian is enjoying the full blessings of their covenant relationship with God. We all know this is true, but why is it true? *It can only be because not every Christian is filled or controlled by the Holy Spirit,* even though they may think they are. They should be and they are commanded to be, but they are now. If they were, the church would have already changed the world.

The Ephesian Power Shortage

This was the problem with the Ephesian Christians. In the first chapter of his letter, Paul reminded the Christians at

Ephesus of how they received the Holy Spirit. He said to them, "In Him [Christ] you also trusted, after you heard the word of truth, the gospel of your salvation; in whom also, having believed, you were sealed with the Holy Spirit of promise" (Ephesians 1:13 NKJ).

Paul came to Ephesus and preached the gospel of Jesus Christ. Many believed and put their trust in Christ. At the moment they believed, Jesus sent the Holy Spirit to live in them and to give them eternal life. They were sealed with the Holy Spirit as we discussed in an earlier chapter. If they would have died, they would have gone right to heaven. In other words, they were saved.

But God wanted to bring heaven down to them right there in Ephesus. By this I mean God desired that the Ephesian Christians would live in the authority and power which Jesus had provided for them. This is why Paul made mention of their spiritual position of being seated with Christ in heavenly places (Ephesians 2:6). They just didn't know who they were in Christ. So before he closed out his letter, Paul told them that they should be filled with the Holy Spirit.

So here we see a group of people who had been born from above (born again) but not filled from above. They have accepted Jesus Christ as their personal Savior, acknowledging Him as the One who died for their sins. They have received the Holy Spirit Who has sealed them into a spiritual union with Christ. Yet Paul told them that God had even more blessings for them. He desired that they be filled or controlled by the Holy Spirit in order to minister and share this glorious life in the Spirit with others.

An Old Testament Example

God gives us a clear picture of this type of situation in the Old Testament. The same Apostle Paul who told the Ephesian Christians to be filled with the Holy Spirit also said that the happenings in the Old Testament are examples from which we are to learn (1 Corinthians 10:6, 11).

So let's examine an Old Testament example that symbolizes in a physical way, the spiritual condition of the Ephesian Christians and many Christians today. The example relates to the cleansing of a leper and is recorded in Leviticus 13-14.

A Fatal Disease

Here's what happened. When a person suspected he had leprosy, he had to go to the High Priest to be examined. Leprosy was a deadly blood disease. It was an internal condition that began deep within and would silently spread until it had defiled and wasted the whole person. It was both hereditary and contagious. It was a disease for which there was no human cure. The leper might live a long time without realizing his condition. But then he would die, passing the leprosy on to his children from one generation to the next.

But the leper suffered something more tragic than the physical suffering. A person who had leprosy was declared to be ceremonially defiled. This means that the leper was not only diseased, but he was also considered unclean. He not only had to be healed, he also had to be cleansed. *This means there was a religious significance attached to leprosy.* Thus the one who had the disease was forced to dwell alone, outside the camp, away from the presence of God, in the place of rejection.

But when God healed a leper, he had once again to be examined by the High Priest. If the High Priest pronounced him healed, he was also declared to be ceremonially clean. He was then allowed back into the camp and the presence of God.

A Strange Anointing

As part of the cleansing ritual, the healed leper would make a sacrifice to God. The High Priest would take the blood of the sacrifice and smear it on the tip of the person's right ear, right thumb and right big toe. *The cleansed leper understood this to mean that God had made him whole and reconciled him unto Himself through the blood.* The person now belonged to God. And through the specific applying of the blood, the cleansed leper was to listen to God's voice (the ear), do His work, (the thumb) and walk in His ways (the toe).

Then the High Priest took some oil and applied it on the blood of the person's right ear, right thumb, and right big toe. *The purpose of applying the oil to the blood was to show that the person was sealed as God's property forever.* The blood had to be applied first. Then the oil was applied to the blood. It symbolically showed that God had cleansed the leper with the blood and sealed him as God's purchased possession through the oil. The application of the oil expressed the person's willingness and desire to listen to God's voice, do His work, and walk in His way.

Left-Over Oil

At this point the High Priest had applied the blood and the oil sealing the person as God's property forever. The leper had been cleansed and reconciled to God. But then the High Priest did something very interesting. *The High Priest had some oil left over. He didn't use it all in the sealing part of the ritual.* And he took the oil and poured it upon the cleansed leper symbolically anointing him with power so that he could listen to God's voice, do His will and walk in His ways.

Spiritual Lepers

Now I'm sure you can see the teaching God has provided through this ritual. In the Bible, leprosy is a type or picture of sin. Like leprosy, sin is an internal condition. It is the Adam-like nature within each of us. Adam passed it down to us and we pass it on to our children from one generation to the next. *We are all spiritual lepers.* We all have a deadly spiritual blood disease for which there is no human cure. It's not only hereditary, but it is also contagious so that we cause others to sin. We can live a long time without realizing our true spiritual condition. But eventually it kills us because the penalty for sin is death (Romans 6:23).

The Perfect Cleansing

Because of our sins, we are separated from God. Like the leper of the Bible, we need to be cleansed of our spiritual leprosy. We need to have our sins forgiven. We need to be reconciled to God. *God's provision for cleansing us is the blood of Jesus Christ.* He is our great High Priest Who pronounces us clean at the cross. The blood of the sacrifice in the cleansing ritual pointed to the perfect sacrifice of Jesus Christ.

The robe of righteousness and the garment of salvation through the blood of Jesus Christ cover us from the top of our head to the soles of our feet. He has made us whole and reconciled us to God through His own blood. Therefore, we are to listen to His voice, do His will and walk in His ways.

The oil in the ritual was symbolic of the Holy Spirit. Jesus, our High Priest, has given us the Holy Spirit. The Holy Spirit comes to live in you sealing you as God's property. *The Holy Spirit works in you the willingness and desire to listen to God's voice, do His work and walk in His way.*

The Better Anointing

At this point, Jesus has applied His blood to your sins at the cross and given you the Holy Spirit so that you now belong to Him. You have been cleansed and reconciled to God. Praise God! You are saved! *But just as the High Priest in the Old Testament had some extra oil, so Jesus desires to pour out a greater measure of His Spirit upon you, anointing you with power so that you can listen to God's voice, do His will and walk in His ways.* In other words, He wants to fill you with the Holy Spirit so that you can minister His life to others.

The Ministry Of Jesus

Jesus Himself had to be filled with the Holy Spirit before He began His ministry. He had to have God's power in His life before He preached, healed the sick, cast out demons, overcame Satan, etc.

Jesus was filled with the Holy Spirit when He was baptized by John in the Jordan River. Matthew recorded the following account: "Then Jesus, when He had been baptized, came up immediately from the water; and behold, the heavens were opened to Him, and He saw the Spirit of God descending like a dove and alighting upon Him. And suddenly a voice came from heaven, saying, 'This is My beloved Son, in whom I am well pleased' " (Matthew 3:16-17 NKJ).

Jesus was now filled with the Holy Spirit. He was ready to begin His ministry. After a brief victorious encounter with Satan, Jesus went to Galilee. The Bible says He went in the power of the Spirit (Luke 4:14).

While in Galilee, Jesus visited His home town of Nazareth. He went to the synagogue and stood up to read the Scriptures. The book of Isaiah was given to Him and He began to read. Here is what He read: "The Spirit of the LORD is upon Me, because He has anointed Me to preach the gospel to the poor. He has sent Me to heal the broken-hearted, to preach deliverance to the captives and recovery of sight to the blind, to set at liberty those who are oppressed, to preach the acceptable year of the Lord"(Luke 4:18-19 NKJ).

A Greater Ministry

Dear reader, this is the ministry of Jesus Christ. This is the great commision that Jesus has given to *all* Christians. He told His followers, "Verily, verily, I say unto you, he that believeth on me, the works that I do shall he do also; and greater works than these shall he do; because I go unto My Father" (John 14:12 KJV).

Jesus said we would do greater things than He did because He was going to the Father. What does going to the Father have to do with us doing greater works than Jesus? It has everything to do with it because when Jesus went to the Father He sent the Holy Spirit upon His disciples. And when the Holy Spirit came upon the disciples, they received power to minister in the Spirit.

Sealed With The Spirit

We see the beginning of this in the Book of Acts. On the evening of His resurrection, Jesus appeared to His followers and gave them the Holy Spirit. John told us what happened, "Then Jesus said to them again, 'Peace to you! As the Father has sent Me, I also send you.' And when He had said this, He breathed on them, and said to them, 'Receive the Holy Spirit' " (John 20:21-22 NKJ).

At that very moment, the disciples received the Holy Spirit Who came to live in them giving them eternal life. *They were born from above but not filled from above.* So Jesus told them to wait until they received the power of God from the filling of the Holy Spirit. Luke recorded these words from Jesus, "Behold, I send the Promise of My Father upon you; but tarry in the city of Jerusalem until you are endued with power from on high" (Luke 24:49 NKJ).

Filled With The Spirit

You would think that if anyone was equipped to minister in the power of the Spirit it would be the disciples. For three years they walked with Jesus. They saw all the miracles He performed. Then they saw Him resurrected from the dead. And they received the Holy Spirit. *But Jesus said He had more for them.* He desired to fill them with the Holy Spirit to give them power to be His witnesses. Luke recorded the fulfillment of this for us which we referred to in Chapter Four. He said, "And they were all filled with the Holy Spirit and began to speak with other tongues, as the Spirit gave them utterance" (Acts 2:4 NKJ).

Peter then stood up with all boldness and gave his great sermon that resulted in three thousand people accepting Jesus as their Lord and being baptized. Peter was not the same big fisherman who earlier hid in fear behind closed doors. He was a different man. He was no longer timid. He was no longer a closet Christian. Neither were the other disciples who were there with him. *It wasn't the resurrection of Jesus that changed them because even after Jesus appeared to them and gave them the Holy Spirit, He still told them to wait.*

Ministering In The Spirit

But after they were filled with the Holy Spirit, they began to minister in the Spirit. They began to minister in the power, authority and boldness of Jesus Christ. This little band of ordinary men and women turned their world upside down. They were the beginning of Jesus' promise that we would do greater works than He did.

You see, when Jesus walked the earth, His ministry was limited to His human body. But now He ministers on planet earth through His spiritual body, the Church. But just as with Jesus and His disciples, we too must be filled with the Holy Spirit. *God still wants to use ordinary men and women to turn the world upside down as we minister in the Spirit.*

Preaching The Gospel

Let's now take a closer look at this ministry in the Spirit. Jesus said that He was anointed to preach the gospel to the poor. He was referring to those who are poor in spirit. *People who are poor in spirit are spiritually bankrupt.* They have nothing they can offer God that will save themselves from their sins. They can draw absolutely nothing from their spiritual bank account to give them eternal life.

The Christian message to these people is, "Blessed are the poor in spirit: for their's is the kingdom of heaven" (Matthew 5:3 KJV). The person who is poor in spirit realizes that he cannot save himself. But he doesn't know how to be saved. The Word of God gives the answer: ". . . by grace are ye saved through faith; and that not of yourselves: it is the gift of God: not of works, lest any man should boast" (Ephesians 2:8-9 KJV).

Paul also wrote to Titus, ". . . when the kindness and the love of God our Savior toward man appeared, not by works of righteousness which we have done, but according to His mercy He saved us, through the washing of regeneration and renewing of the Holy Spirit, whom He poured out on us abundantly through Jesus Christ our Savior, that having been justified [declared righteous] by His grace we should become heirs according to the hope of eternal life" (Titus 3:4-7 NKJ).

Christians have the answer for those who are poor in spirit. The answer is, "Today, God's grace is extended to you through faith in Jesus Christ. Today, God desires to take away your heart of stone and give you a heart of flesh. He desires to put His Spirit within you and write His laws on the fleshly tablets of your heart. He desires to forgive your iniquities and remember them no more. He desires to give you eternal life."

Healing The Brokenhearted

Jesus said He was sent to heal the brokenhearted. The world is full of people who are brokenhearted. Their lives have been shattered by the harshness, injustices and pressures of the world. And they don't know how to put their lives back together.

The Christian message to the brokenhearted is, "Blessed are they that mourn: for they shall be comforted" (Matthew 5:4 KJV).

Jesus also said, "Come unto me, all ye that labour and are heavy laden, and I will give you rest. Take my yoke upon you, and learn of me; for I am meek and lowly in heart: and ye shall find rest unto your souls. For my yoke is easy, and my burden is light" (Matthew 11:28-30 KJV).

Jesus spoke these words as well, "Peace I leave with you, my peace I give unto you: not as the world giveth, give I unto you. Let not your heart be troubled, neither let it be afraid . . . these things I have spoken unto you, that in me ye might have peace. In the world ye shall have tribulation: but be of good cheer; I have overcome the world" (John 14:27; 16:33 KJV).

Christians have the words of life for those who are brokenhearted. The Prophet Isaiah spoke these comforting words from God: "Fear thou not; for I am with thee: be not

84

dismayed; for I am thy God: I will strengthen thee; yea, I will help thee; yea, I will uphold thee with the right hand of my righteousness" (Isaiah 41:10 KJV).

God specializes in healing the brokenhearted. When we come to Jesus, He puts our lives back together again. This is why Paul wrote, "Therefore, if anyone is in Christ, he is a new creation; old things have passed away; behold, all things have become new" (2 Corinthians 5:17 NKJ).

Setting Captives Free

Jesus preached deliverance to the captives. As we learned in an earlier chapter, all of us are held captive by our old Adam-like nature. We are slaves to our self-destructive sin nature. No matter how hard people try, they cannot break the chains of sin that hold them captive.

The Christian message to those in bondage to sin is, "Whom the Son sets free is free indeed . . . walk in the Spirit and you shall not fulfill the lusts of the flesh." (See John 8:36; 2 Corinthians 3:17; Galatians 5:16.)

God desires that you be set free from the chains of sin. He has broken these chains through the death and resurrection of Jesus Christ. The prison door is open. All you have to do is walk through it by faith in Jesus Christ.

Bringing Sight To The Blind

The Bible says that Satan blinds the minds of people to keep them in spiritual darkness (2 Corinthians 4:4). Well-meaning people, struggling to do their best, walk in spiritual darkness and don't even know it. They can't see that the light of the knowledge of the glory of God shines in the face of Jesus Christ (2 Corinthians 4:6). So they stumble through life not knowing where they are going nor how to get there.

The Christian message to the spiritually blind is that "Jesus is the light of the world." Light gives life and sight. Jesus gives us eternal life. He opens our spiritual eyes and helps us to see what God is like and how we can know Him and walk with Him.

85

Jesus shares His light with all who will come to Him (John 8:12). We become his light-bearers. He said it this way in Matthew: "You are the light of the world. A city that is set on a hill cannot be hidden. Nor do they light a lamp and put it under a basket, but on a lampstand, and it gives light to all who are in the house. Let your light so shine before men, that they may see your good works and glorify your Father who is in heaven" (Matthew 5:14-16 NKJ).

When Christians walk in the light, people who are lost in darkness will be able to see God's salvation for them in Jesus. They will no longer be disoriented. They will no longer wander in the darkness of this world trying to find their way out. They will come to the glorious light of life in Jesus and bear that same light themselves so that others will be able to see the glory of God.

Liberating The Oppressed

Luke wrote "how God anointed Jesus of Nazareth with the Holy Spirit and with power, who went about doing good and healing all who were oppressed by the devil, for God was with Him" (Acts 10:38 NKJ).

Satan is an oppresser. As the god of this world system, he crushes people under the heavy weight of his rule. People become depressed. They get despondent. They give up. They lose hope. They turn to alcohol or drugs to numb their mind, thinking this will help them cope or forget their despair.

The Christian message for the oppressed is that Jesus has destroyed the power of Satan (Colossians 2:15). We no longer have to serve him. We no longer have to be intimidated and beat down by his cruel and harsh ways.

God has liberated us from the power of Satan through Jesus Christ. So when you come to Christ, His victory becomes yours. And then greater is He (the Holy Spirit) Who is in you than he (Satan) who is in the world (1 John 4:4).

86

Proclaiming The Year Of The Lord

Finally, Jesus said He came to preach the acceptable year of the Lord. By this, Jesus meant "now is the time for our salvation." You see, when Jesus came the first time to planet earth, He came as the Lamb of God to take away our sins. But when He comes the second time, He will come as the Lion from the tribe of Judah to judge our sins. Then it will be too late to be saved.

The Christian message for the world is, "Today is the acceptable year of the Lord. Today God's grace is extended to you. Now is the time for your salvation. Now is the time to turn from your sins and find forgiveness and eternal life in Jesus Christ."

Jesus said it this way, "For God so loved the world, that he gave his only begotten Son, that whosoever believeth in him should not perish, but have everlasting life. For God sent not his Son into the world to condemn the world; but that the world through him might be saved" (John 3:16-17 KJV).

It's Your Ministry

This is what it means to minister in the Spirit. It is the very ministry of Jesus Christ on planet earth through His spiritual body, the Church. *This is not a work just for the pastor or a few spiritual elite. This is what all Christians are to be doing as they go about their daily lives.* The pastor equips the Church with the Word of God so that the Church can go into the world and minister in the Spirit, sharing the life of Jesus Christ with others.

God desires that *all Christians* be able to say, "The Spirit of the Lord is upon me, because He has anointed me to preach the gospel to the poor. He has sent me to heal the brokenhearted, to preach deliverance to the captives, recovery of sight to the blind, to set at liberty those who are oppressed and to preach the acceptable year of the Lord."

How To Be Filled

The disciples were initially filled with the Holy Spirit on the Day of Pentecost. *But this was more than just a one-time*

87

experience, both for them and for us. It is a way of life. The Holy Spirit is not an "it." He is a divine personality Who comes to live in you as a complete person. Therefore, you don't get more of the Holy Spirit as you would some vague, abstract feeling such as the school spirit, for example. Instead, the Holy Spirit gets more of you.

As you respond to the Holy Spirit, He renews your mind so that you think as Christ thinks. He brings stability and the peace of God to your emotions. He changes the desires of your heart so that your will is to do those things that are pleasing to God. The result is that the Holy Spirit rules over your soul, filling you with His presence and controlling your every word, thought and deed.

This is a relationship with God that you must desire more than anything of the world. Jesus put it this way: "Blessed are they which do hunger and thirst after righteousness: for they shall be filled" (Matthew 5:6 KJV). Do you hunger and thirst for more of God in your life? Have you set your affections on Him? Do you sense the power of God in your life? Are you ministering in the Spirit? If you must honestly answer "no" to these questions, I pray that you can see this is God's desire for you. And there's no better time than the present for you to be filled with the Holy Spirit. All you have to do is ask. *Have you asked Him? Will you ask Him now?*

Jesus said, "And I say to you, ask and it will be given to you; seek, and you will find; knock, and it will be opened to you. For everyone who asks receives, and he who seeks finds, and to him who knocks it will be opened. If a son asks for bread from any father among you, will he give him a stone? Or if he asks for a fish, will he give him a serpent instead of a fish? Of if he asks for an egg, will he offer him a scorpion? If you then, being evil, know how to give good gifts to your children, how much more will your heavenly Father give the Holy Spirit to those who ask Him!" (Luke 11:9-13 NKJ).

Review Exercise 5

1. Explain the difference between receiving the indwelling of the Holy Spirit and being filled with the Holy Spirit.

2. What is the purpose of being filled with the Holy Spirit?

3. Why is it important to be filled with the Holy Spirit?

4. How do you become filled with the Holy Spirit?

5. How can you apply this knowledge to your life?

Lust/Flesh
hunger -
thirst - sex
feels good

Lust EYES
"I want it -
at looks good".

PRIDE OF LIFE
Power
Control.

7
Wearing The Armor

Immediately after Jesus was filled with the Spirit, He encountered spiritual warfare in the desert, after fasting for forty days and forty nights. As Jesus drew near to God in preparation for His ministry, Satan came to tempt Him. Yet Jesus overcame Satan's temptations. *He overcame Satan because He understood and knew how to carry on spiritual warfare.* After defeating Satan, His fame soon spread throughout the region as He began to minister in the power of the Holy Spirit. (See Luke 4:1-5.)

Once we are filled with the Holy Spirit, we too will be tempted by Satan in ways that we've never before known. The closer we draw near to God, the more our spiritual battles intensify. We become a threat to Satan when we begin to minister in the Spirit. He will do anything he can to defeat us. In order to overcome him, we too must understand and know how to carry on spiritual warfare.

91

As we are successful in overcoming Satan, people will also notice us and come to us for help, as they did with Jesus.

In this chapter, we are going to learn how to wear the armor of God so that we can be successful in our spiritual battles. In doing so, we're going to find out as much as we can about our enemy (Satan), his battle plans, and the types of weapons he uses. Then we will learn about the weapons God has provided for us as Christians and how to effectively use them to stand in the victory God has already given us in Jesus Christ.

The Real Enemy

Let's begin by identifying our real enemy. The Bible says it's the *devil*. Paul wrote to the Ephesian Christians, "Finally, my brethren, be strong in the Lord and in the power of His might. Put on the whole armor of God, that you may be able to stand against the wiles of the devil. For we do not wrestle against flesh and blood, but against principalities, against powers, against the rulers of the darkness of this age, against spiritual hosts of wickedness in the heavenly places" (Ephesians 6:10-12 NKJ).

Paul told us that our real enemy is the devil and the great host of demon followers that make up his army. Satan has organized his demon army into a chain of command which Paul referred to as principalities, powers, rulers of darkness and spiritual wickedness. *Satan's objective is to establish a one-world system through which he will rule planet earth and be worshipped as God.* He seeks to evangelize humanity to his counterfeit kingdom called the world system. Satan makes war against Christians because we know his plan, and we hinder him from accomplishing it as we minister in the Spirit.

Satan's Origin And Fall

Many people doubt the reality of a literal, personal devil. To many, the devil is just a character out of the imagination of man's mind. They think of him as a strange character running around in a red suit with a long tail, horns and pitchfork. This image came about in the Middle Ages when the devil was portrayed in plays. The person portraying the devil was always costumed in this way so that the audience could recognize the character as being the devil. But nothing could be further from the truth about what the devil is really like. There really is a devil and a spirit world that we cannot comprehend with our physical senses.

The Bible is our only source book of truth concerning the devil and this spirit world. There are two particular references in the Bible that give us a glimpse of Satan's origin and fall. These are Ezekiel 28:12-19 and Isaiah 14:10-16. It would be helpful for you to read these Scripture references. I want to briefly explain them for you.

The Bible tells us that Satan was at one time called Lucifer. Lucifer means "light-bearer." Lucifer was God's most perfect, splendid creation. He was the top ranking angel and served at God's throne. He was very beautiful so that his outward appearance was iridescent, like a magnificent rainbow reflecting the glory of God.

When God created Lucifer, He created him perfect. People often say, "How can there be a devil? God couldn't create an evil creature like the devil. So there must not be a devil." Part of this reasoning is correct. God can't create anything that is evil. And He didn't create Lucifer as an evil creature. *He created Lucifer as a perfect angelic creature for the purpose of serving Him and reflecting His divine glory.*

But that wasn't good enough for Lucifer. He wanted more. He wanted to be worshipped as God. So he led a rebellion in heaven against God. He convinced a third of the angels to join with him in an attempt to overthrow God and place himself on the throne of the universe (Jude 6; 2 Peter 2:4; Revelation 12:4, 9). Lucifer himself introduced evil into the universe through the sin of pride.

But of course God could not tolerate this rebellion. He was forced to banish Lucifer from His presence. Lucifer then became known as Satan or the devil. The angels that followed Lucifer became his demonic army. They seek to deceive humans into worshipping Satan through the world system that Satan is the God of and in which we live. *This will find its climax in the end times when the unbelieving world will worship Satan through the antichrist who will be ruling over a one-world religious-political-military-economic system.* They will acknowledge their worship of Satan by taking the mark of the beast (antichrist). (See Revelation 9:20-21, 13.)

Satan's Present Position

The word Satan means "adversary." Satan, who was once God's closest creation, is now the adversary (enemy) of God and man. He has established a world system on planet earth. This world system is expressed through the philosophies, attitudes, attractions, ways and means of the world. The Bible says that Satan is the God of this world system (2 Corinthians 4:4; Ephesians 2:2; John 12:31, 14:30, 16:11; 1 John 5:18-19). It is a system of antichrist. *Satan desires to live out his god-image by ruling over his world system.* People actually worship him as they give themselves to the world system. This is why the Bible says, "Do not love the world or the things in the world" (1 John 2:15 NKJ).

Satan's Future

The Bible also teaches that one day Jesus Christ will return to planet earth and destroy this world system established by Satan. At that time, Satan will be bound for a thousand years in the bottomless pit and a new world system will be established. Jesus Christ will rule over this new world system with perfect justice and righteousness. Then, after a brief reprieve, Satan, his demon army and all who worship him through their love of his world system will be cast into hell forever. (See Revelation 19-20.) Until that time, God allows Satan to rule over this present world system and conduct guerrilla warfare against Christians.

Satan's Character

The Bible gives us a description of Satan's character. Here are some of the things it says about him:

94

Satan desires to sift you as wheat (Luke 22:31).

Satan is like a roaring lion seeking to devour you (1 Peter 5:8).

Satan is the father of lies and a murderer from the beginning (John 8:44).

Satan possesses wily (crafty) ways (Ephesians 6:11).

Satan disguises himself as an angel of light (2 Corinthians 11:4, 13-15).

Satan is a deceiver (Revelation 12:9).

Satan accuses (condemns) Christians (Revelation 12:10).

Satan causes spiritual blindness (2 Corinthians 4:4).

Satan keeps people from believing the gospel (Matthew 13:9).

Satan is a sinner and lures us to sin (1 John 3:8).

In the Bible, Satan is said to make people sick, blind, unable to talk, insane and suicidal. Jesus compared him to a thief who comes to steal, kill and destory (John 10:10). *Satan has his own counterfeit religion with counterfeit preachers and a counterfeit gospel* (1 Timothy 4:1-2; 2 Timothy 3:5, 4:3; 2 Corinthians 11:13-15). The very first demon-possessed person Jesus encountered was sitting in the church house (Mark 1:23-26).

Satan's Defeat
Yes, Satan is a real personality. He is our enemy. And the real battles we face are of a spiritual nature. *But wouldn't it be great if you could go into battle knowing that your enemy is already defeated?* Wouldn't it be great if you knew beforehand that you would win? Then you wouldn't have to be afraid of your enemy.

Well, the Bible says that Satan is already defeated (Colossians 2:15; Hebrews 2:14). Jesus defeated him by His resurrection. And, as we've learned in previous chapters, Jesus' victory is ours as Christians, through our personal identification with Him in all He did on our behalf.

You see, as Christians, we aren't just winning. We have already won! We're seated with Christ in heavenly places with authority and power over Satan, over sin and the fear of death. *We don't defeat Satan ourselves; Jesus has already defeated him for us.* Satan's whole campaign against Christians is just a bluff. But he gets away with it because most Christians don't realize their victorious position in Christ. They are not aware of the victory Christ has already won for them.

So how do you prepare for battle against an enemy that is already defeated? Well, you just put on your armor, claim your victory and demand that your enemy surrender. This is just what we Christians must do to tell the devil that we know who we are in Christ. But to do so, we must know how to put on and wear the spiritual armor God has given us. Let's now see what this armor is and how to use it against the devil.

The Christian's Armor

When Paul wrote the Ephesian Christians about spiritual warfare, he told them that their strength and power was from God. He was speaking of the authority God had given them in Christ. He then pointed out that their armor was the armor of God. It was not their armor. He said it this way to the Corinthians, "For though we walk in the flesh, we do not war according to the flesh. For the weapons of our warfare are not carnal but mighty in God for pulling down strongholds " (2 Corinthians 10:3-4 NKJ).

This was Paul's way of telling us that God is our source. God has defeated Satan for us through Jesus Christ. So we don't have to defeat the devil ourselves. *We simply "stand" in the victory God has already won for us.* We do this by putting on the whole armor of God. Paul described this armor for us. He wrote, "Therefore take up the whole armor of God, that you may be able to withstand in the evil day, and having done all, to stand. Stand therefore, having girded your waist with truth, having put on the breastplate of righteousness, and having shod your feet with the preparation of the gospel of peace; above all, taking the shield of faith with which you will be able to quench all the fiery darts of the wicked ones. And take the helmet of salvation, and the sword of the Spirit, which is the word of God; praying always with all prayer and supplication in the Spirit, being watchful to this end with all perseverance and supplication for all the saints" (Ephesians 6:13-18 NKJ).

Paul mentioned six pieces of armor. *Each piece of armor represents an aspect of Christ Himself. Taken as a whole, they give us a symbolic description of the person and completed work of Jesus in defeating Satan for us.* Here's how Paul expressed this point to the Romans: ". . . put on the Lord Jesus Christ, and make no provision for the flesh, to fulfill its lusts" (Romans 13:14 NKJ).

So you see, Jesus is our armor. He is our armor because He has defeated Satan. And His victory becomes ours as we allow Him to live His life through us. *The Christian's armor is simply Christ in us, living His life out of us with the result being that His victory over Satan becomes ours.* This armor, as a description of Christ, shows us how to allow Christ to appropriate His victory for us in our everyday lives as we live in the Spirit. Let's now briefly examine each piece of the armor and see how to practically apply this knowledge to our lives.

Belt Of Truth

First, Paul mentioned the *belt of truth.* The Roman soldier wore a type of skirt that was very similar to a Scottish kilt. Then, over the skirt, he wore a loose-fitting garment which was tied at the middle by a girdle, or, as we would say, a belt. This belt was about six to eight inches wide. It was the most important part of the soldier's armor because all of his weapons were fastened to it. When the Roman soldier went into battle, he would tuck the loose-fitting garment up in his belt to give himself complete freedom to move about. If the Roman soldier was told, "gird up your loins," he would tuck his garment up in his belt as preparation to fight. Likewise, the Christian belt that holds our armor together and prepares us to fight the devil is truth.

Now we've just noted in our description of Satan's character that he possesses wily ways. This means that he is clever, crafty and cunning. *So he fights us with lying deceptions.* He uses them to disarm us. We see his lying deceptions in the philosophies of the world Satan has given us so many different philosophies that men and women are confused, not knowing where they came from, what they are doing or where they are going. The world has lost touch with reality and truth.

And all along the way, the devil is whispering in our ears, "All you need to find truth is to enroll in Philosophy 101 in college, go to a hidden mountain retreat and sit at the feet of some Eastern guru, make a lot of money, obtain power, fame and success, take some mind-expanding drug, experiment with sex. The Bible is a bunch of fairy tales for old women and kids, religion is opium for the masses, everything is relative, we're all God's children, sin in moderation is respectable, if it feels good do it, God helps those who help themselves, surely a loving God would never banish you from His presence." By the time someone discovers this is not true, Satan has already defeated him over and over again.

The word "truth" means "reality." When Jesus stood before Pilate, the Roman governor, He said, "I have come to bear witness to the truth." Pilate responded by saying, "What is truth?" (See John 18:37-38.) Pilate was one of the leading politicians of the greatest, most powerful nation of his day. He had all the privileges of power, education and influence. Yet he had to admit to Jesus that he just didn't know what was real. He was confused by the lying deceptions of the devil.

In John 14:6 *Jesus said that He was truth.* He didn't

just teach truth, but He Himself was truth in the flesh. By this Jesus meant that through Him we learn the reality of God, our relationship to Him and the world in which we live. He shows us things as they really are and life as it really is. Through Him we see our need for salvation and reconciliation to God. By Him we find forgiveness and eternal life at the cross.

The Christian has seen a revelation from God that Jesus Christ is truth. He is reality. He is the real thing. If you drink from His well, you will never thirst again. Because He gives meaning and purpose to life. In Him are hidden all the treasures of wisdom and knowledge (Colossians 2:3).

When we come to Christ, we receive the Holy Spirit Who is called the Spirit of truth. *When we live in the Spirit, He will guide us into truth so that we won't be deceived by Satan's lies.* (See John 16:13.) Instead of everything being grey, everything will be black and white. We will see things clearly. We will be able to determine right from wrong, truth from lies, reality from fantasy.

John wrote these words to a man named Gaius: "For I rejoiced greatly when brethren came and testified of the truth that is in you, just as you walk in the truth. I have no greater joy than to hear that my children walk in truth" (3 John 3-4 NKJ).

Jesus said it this way: "If you abide in My word, you are My disciples indeed. And you shall know the truth, and the truth shall make you free" (John 8:31-32 NKJ). We are set free from Satan's lying deceptions when we walk in the truth as God has revealed it to us by Christ Jesus.

Breastplate Of Righteousness

The next piece of armor is the *breastplate of righteousness.* The roman solider wore a breastplate made of bronze or chains that covered his body from his neck to his waist. Thus, it protected the most vulnerable part of the soldier's body, his heart.

Satan knows this is where we are most vulnerable. *As the accuser of the brethren, he tries to condemn us and make* us feel guilty. He is always bringing up our past sins. He is always putting us down. He is constantly pointing out our failures. He wants us to think that God's favor towards us is dependent on our living perfect lives. And since he knows we don't live perfect lives, he uses this to convince us that we are such failures that God has given up on us. He's negative—negative—negative!

The devil knows that if he can make us feel guilty and put us under condemnation, we will throw up our hands and want to give up trying to walk with God. We'll become so discouraged that we'll stop reading our Bible. We'll stop praying because we'll feel unworthy. We won't fellowship with other Christians because we'll feel guilty around them. And before we know what's hit us, Satan will have pierced our hearts.

So we defend ourselves with the breastplate of righteousness. But how do we do this? We do this by realizing that it is Christ's righteousness through which we find favor with God. The word righteous means "right standing." We have right standing with God through Jesus Christ. *It's not our righteousness; it is His.*

Paul wrote to the Corinthians that Jesus is our righteousness (1 Corinthians 1:30). On another occasion, he told them, "For [God] made Him [Christ] who knew no sin to be sin for us, that we might become the righteousness of God in Him" (2 Corinthians 5:21 NKJ).

Jesus never sinned. Therefore, He was perfectly righteous in the sight of God. When we accept Jesus as our Savior, God credits the righteousness of Jesus to our account. *So our relationship with God is not based on our own righteousness. It is based on the righteousness of Jesus Christ.*

Jesus said in John 5:24, "Verily, verily, I say unto you, he that heareth my word, and believeth on him that sent me, hath everlasting life, and shall not come into condemnation; but is passed from death unto life" (KJV).

Paul wrote to the Romans, "There is therefore now no condemnation to those who are in Christ Jesus, who do not walk according to the flesh, but according to the Spirit" (Romans 8:1 KJV). In that same chapter, he added these words: "Who shall bring a charge against God's elect? It is God who justifies [declares right]. Who is he who condemns? It is Christ who died, and furthermore is also risen, who is even at the right hand of God, who also makes intercession for us" (Romans 8:33-34 NKJ).

There is no one, including the devil, who can condemn us who are Christians. We don't stand against him with our own righteousness but with the righteousness of Jesus Christ. The next time Satan tries to make you feel guilty, you remind him that you are standing against him with the righteousness of Jesus Christ. God has accepted you in Christ Jesus. You stand complete in Him.

Shoes Of Peace

Paul now mentions the next piece of armor, *the shoes of peace.* The Roman soldier was constantly in hand-to-hand combat. Sure footing was a must. He had to keep his balance. One slip and he would be dead. To ensure firm footing, the Roman soldier drove nails in the soles of his sandals. As he fought, the nails dug into the ground, enabling him to keep his balance.

Satan would like to knock us off balance with fear and worry. He would have us worry about everything: our job, our health, our finances, our kids, our parents, food, clothing, and shelter. He wants us to be tense, nervous, uptight and anxious. That way we are no good to God, ourselves or anybody else. Satan has knocked some people so far off balance that they worry when they don't have anything to worry about.

Jesus is our peace (Ephesians 2:14). We have peace with God through Him (Romans 5:1). Jesus not only gives us peace with God, He also gives us the peace of God. He said to His disciples, "Peace I leave with you, My peace I give to you; not as the world gives do I give to you. Let not your heart be troubled, neither let it be afraid. . . .

These things I have spoken to you, that in Me you may have peace. In the world you will have tribulation; but be of good cheer, I have overcome the world" (John 14:27, 16:33 NKJ).

Paul wrote to the Philippian Christians, "Be anxious for nothing, but in everything by prayer and supplication, with thanksgiving, let your requests be made known to God; and the peace of God, which surpasses all understanding, will guard your hearts and minds through Christ Jesus" (Philippians 4:6-7 NKJ).

Paul spoke about the peace of God. All Christians have peace with God, but not all Christians enjoy the peace of God. Satan has knocked them off balance with fear and worry. But you can have the peace of God as you live in the Spirit. *The Holy Spirit will bring peace and stability (firm footing) to your emotions.* God's peace will be like a guard protecting both your heart and mind from fear and worry.

Isaiah told us the means for peace. He said that God Himself will keep us in perfect peace as we keep our minds on Him (Isiaah 26:3). You don't have to be fearful and worrisome. God will meet your every need as you put your trust in Him. May you know His peace that passes all understanding. Cast your cares upon Him, for He cares for you. Seek first the kingdom of God and all these other things shall be added unto you.

Shield Of Faith

Then we have the *shield of faith.* The Roman soldier's shield was about two feet wide and four feet long. He used it to protect himself against the enemy arrows that frequently were set on fire at the tip before being discharged. The edges of his shield were so constructed that an entire line of soldiers could interlock their shields to block the fiery arrows.

Satan's fiery dart is doubt. First of all, he tries to get us to doubt God's Word. You remember, this was his tactic against Eve. He put doubts in Eve's mind about the truth of God's Word. He attempts to get us to doubt that God even exists. He wants us to doubt Chritianity in general and our salvation specifically. He tells us we can't overcome sin, himself and death. He makes us think we can't have a victorious Christian life. He wants us to be so unsure of our relationship with God that we come to the point where we say, "I guess I've just lost my faith." And that is just what Satan wants to hear.

But dear friend, if you are a Christian, you haven't lost your faith. Do you know why you haven't? *Because Jesus is the author and finisher of your faith.* (See Hebrews 12:2.)

You see, it's the faith of God that has been given to you. The faith of God will never fail. You may not always properly hide behind it for protection, but it's always there. *We don't live by feelings; we live by faith.*

Consider Peter, for example. One day Jesus said to Peter, "Simon, Simon! Indeed, Satan has asked for you, that he may sift you as wheat. But I have prayed for you, that your faith should not fail . . ." (Luke 22:31-32 NKJ).

Peter then went and denied Jesus three times. I'm sure that at that moment and thereafter he had many doubts. I'm sure he hated himself. I'm sure he thought he had lost his faith. Satan was sifting him as wheat. But Jesus prayed that his faith would not fail. A short time later, Peter recovered from his doubts and preached a great sermon that resulted in three thousand people accepting Jesus as their Lord.

We may, at times, deny Jesus. We may not always do just the right thing. Satan will try to sift us as wheat. This may cause us to doubt. But Jesus is praying that your faith will not fail. Has Jesus ever said a prayer that the Father didn't positively answer? Do you think God is going to answer this prayer from Jesus on your behalf? Then is your faith going to fail? Of course not!

So what do you do when you have doubts? You simply say, "Devil, you are a liar! I haven't lost my faith. Jesus is the author and finisher of my faith, and He has prayed that my faith will not fail."

John said it this way: ". . . whatever is born of God overcomes the world. And this is the victory that has overcome the world—our faith. Who is he who overcomes the world, but he who believes Jesus is the Son of God" (1 John 5:4-5 NKJ).

Helmet Of Salvation

The next piece of armor is the *helmet of salvation.* The Roman soldier's helmet protected his head. It was a vital piece of his armor. As long as he had on his helmet, he could withstand the heaviest of blows.

Likewise, we need the helmet of salvation to protect our mind against Satan's blows. Paul told us in 1 Thessalonians 5:8 that the helmet of salvation is the helmet of *hope.*

You see, the devil wants you to believe that the world is out of control. He wants you to believe that the world situation is dark and gloomy. He wants you to think that we all are going to blow ourselves up. He tells you God can't do anything about it. Therefore, there is no hope. And if there is no hope, you might as well give up in *despair and depression.* As some would say today, "Tune in, turn on, drop out. Don't take responsibility. Give your mind to drugs, your body to sex and go up in the mountains somewhere and freak out."

Well beloved of God, the Bible says there is hope. The Bible says there is a sovereign God Who is actively ruling over the universe. He is moving the course of world events for His glory and the good of His children. He has a plan which He is carrying out and He is right on schedule. As part of His plan, He gives man a limited amount of freedom. But He alone is absolutely free, and, out of His absolute freedom, He overrides evil and uses it to further His purposes.

The biblical meaning of the word "hope" is not just wishful thinking. It is a joyful expectation and anticipation of the good that God has promised. *The hope which God has given His children is that Jesus will come for us, and we will*

live with Him forever in a glorified body where there will be
no more tears, no more death, neither sorrow, nor crying,
neither shall there be any more pain (Revelation 21:1-4).

Jesus said in John 14:1-3, "Let not your heart be troubled;
you believe in God, believe also in Me. In My Father's house
are many mansions; if it were not so, I would have told you. I
go to prepare a place for you. And if I go and prepare a place
for you, I will come again and receive you to Myself; that
where I am, there you may be also" (NKJ).

Paul wrote of this to the Thessalonians. He said, ". . . I do
not want you to be ignorant, brethren, concerning those
who have fallen asleep, lest you sorrow as others who have
no hope. For if we believe that Jesus died and rose again,
even so God will bring with Him those who sleep in Jesus.
For this we say to you by the word of the Lord, that we who
are alive and remain until the coming of the Lord will by no
means precede those who are asleep. For the Lord Himself
will descend from heaven with a shout, with the voice of an
archangel, and with the trumpet of God. And the dead in
Christ will rise first. Then we who are alive and remain shall
be caught up together with them in the clouds to meet the
Lord in the air. And thus we shall always be with the Lord.
Therefore comfort one another with these words" (1
Thessalonians 4:13-18 NKJ).

He wrote to the Corinthians, "Behold, I tell you a
mystery: We shall not all sleep, but we shall all be
changed—in a moment, in the twinkling of an eye, at the
last trumpet. For the trumpet will sound, and the dead will
be raised incorruptible, and we shall be changed. For this
corruptible must put on incorruption, and this mortal must
put on immortality. So when this corruptible has put on
incorruption, and this mortal has put on immortality, then
shall be brought to pass the saying that is written: *"Death is
swallowed up in victory." "O Death, where is your sting? O
Hades, where is your victory?"* The sting of death is sin, and
the strength of sin is the law. But thanks be to God, who
gives us the victory through our Lord Jesus Christ.
Therefore, my beloved brethren, be steadfast, immovable,

always abounding in the work of the Lord, knowing that your labor is not in vain in the Lord"(1 Corinthians 15:51-58 NKJ).

Christian friend, your labor is not in vain. You have a hope. *Jesus is your hope.* (1 Timothy 1:1). You have a grand future ahead of you. Christ in you is your hope of glory (Colossians 1:27). The next time Satan attacks your mind, you remind him of the glorious future God has prepared for you. As Paul wrote to the Romans, "I reckon that the sufferings of this present time are not worthy to be compared with the glory which shall be revealed in us" (Romans 8:18 KJV).

Sword Of The Spirit

The last piece of armor is the *sword of the Spirit*. The Roman sword was an awesome weapon. It was about two feet long, sharp on both edges and pointed on the end. The Roman solider, skilled in the use of his sword, could quickly dispose of his enemy.

Paul compared the Word of God to the Roman sword. It is an awesome weapon in the hands of a Christian who knows how to use it. As you become skilled in its use, you can quickly dispose of your enemy, the devil.

The writer of Hebrews put it this way: ". . . the word of God is living and powerful, and sharper than any two-edged sword, piercing even to the division of soul and spirit, and of joints and marrow, and is a discerner of the thoughts and intents of the heart" (Hebrews 4:12 NKJ).

Satan will tempt you to disobey the Word of God. This was his strategy against Jesus. But each time Satan tempted Jesus, He responded with the Word of God. (See Luke 4:1-14.) Finally, Satan gave up for a while and left Jesus alone. Jesus knew how to use the Word of God to dispose of the devil.

We must learn how to use it as well. First of all, *we must realize that it is not our sword, but it is the sword of the Spirit.* Now it's very important that you understand what

106

Paul meant by the phrase "the sword of the Spirit." I want to try to explain it to you.

The New Testament was written in the Greek language. The Greek language was much more expressive than the English language is. Its words had very precise meanings. *In the New Testament there are two different Greek words translated into the English Bible that are referred to by the phrase "The Word of God."*

The first of these Greek words is *logos*. This word refers to the general revelation of God in its entirety. Thus the whole Bible may be referred to as the Word of God. It is the general written revelation from God for everybody.

The second of these Greek words is *rhema*. This word refers to a specific personal revelation from God to an individual. It is the spoken Word of God by the Holy Spirit to you personally. This is a situation in which the Holy Spirit takes the general logos of God (the Bible) which was written for everybody and makes specific Scriptures come alive to you personally. When this happens, you know that God has spoken to you personally. You have received a "Thus saith the Lord" in your spirit.

When Paul spoke about the sword of the Spirit being the Word of God, he used the word "rhema." So, in this instance, he was not referring to the Bible as the written Word of God. But he was talking about the "rhema" Word of God which the Holy Spirit quickens to your heart on an individual basis. It is a revelation from the Holy Spirit to you personally for guidance, comfort, wisdom, and for bringing Scripture to your remembrance in time of need, such as spiritual warfare against Satan.

A lot of people know the Bible and can quote many verses from it. Yet they are weak. The reason is they have the logos of God in their head, but they've not gotten the rhema from God in their heart. Others try to claim Scriptures for themselves that the Holy Spirit has never spoken to them personally. They are talking from their head, not their heart. Even though they are repeating Scripture, it's not the sword of the Spirit until the Holy Spirit makes it come alive to them personally.

When Jesus spoke the Word of God to Satan, He said, "It is written, 'Man shall not live by bread alone, but by every word that proceeds from the mouth of God' " (Matthew 4:4 NKJ). The Greek word used to record Jesus' statement is "rhema." Jesus was talking about the personal word from God quickened to your heart by the Holy Spirit. He even went on to describe this word as coming from the mouth of God. *It's the spoken Word of God by the Holy Spirit that enables us to speak with authority and power against Satan.*

Jesus is the Word of God (John 1:1-3, 14; Revelation 19:13). As you learn to meditate on Him and His words, the Holy Spirit will make them come alive to you personally. You will begin to hear the voice of God speaking to your heart. Whatever God speaks to your heart, you confess with your mouth. As you confess that word (rhema) with your mouth, Satan will leave you alone.

Christ Is Our Armor

This is the Christian armor. And it's so important to realize and remember that this is not armor we get from God, but we get God Himself Who is our armor. When Satan gives you a lying deception, you will be prepared to fight his lies through Jesus, Who is your truth. When Satan accuses you with guilt and condemnation, you protect yourself through Jesus, Who is your righteousness. The next time Satan tries to knock you off balance through fear and worry, remember that Jesus is your peace. When Satan fires arrows of doubt at you, you block them through Jesus, Who is your faith. You can overcome Satan's blows of despair and depression through Jesus, Who is your hope. And finally, you resist Satan's temptations by relying on Jesus, the Word of God.

Paul went on to mention that none of this armor is really effective without prayer. And even our prayers are in the name of Jesus. *To pray in the name of Jesus means to pray in the character of Jesus.* We are able to pray in the character of

Jesus as we live in His character. When we seek to live in His character, the Holy Spirit exercises Christ's authority through us over Satan.

So yes, there really is a devil. There really is a spirit world. There really are spiritual battles. Satan is your enemy. You cannot defeat him with your own strength. But Jesus Christ has defeated him for you. He desires to clothe you with His garment of salvation and robe of righteousness which is His very own life. He is your armor. I pray that you will put Him on and wear Him. May you be strong in the Lord and the power of His might.

As the Apostle James wrote, "Submit yourselves therefore to God. Resist the devil and he will flee from you. Draw near to God and he will draw near to you" (James 4:7-8 RSV). This we are able to do as we put on the whole armor of God and stand in the victory of Christ.

Review Exercise 6

1. Give a brief description of the career of Satan and what he is trying to accomplish.

2. List the six pieces of the Christian armor and how each relates to Christ.

   a.

   b.

   c.

   e.

   e.

   f.

3. How can you apply this knowledge to your life?

8
Living As Christ's Disciple

When we study the ministry of Jesus, we quickly begin to realize that He did not just seek converts. He did not just ask people to casually believe in Him. Nor did He call people to a religious organization or experience. Neither did He ask them to all agree to a certain creed. But He had something much more demanding in mind. *He called people to a way of life.* He challenged men and women to forsake their own lives and follow Him. *He called people to be His disciples.* This is still His call today.

It's only when we live as Christ's disciples that our position in heavenly places becomes our real life experience on planet earth, so it is only fitting that we close out this book by examining what it really means to live as Christ's disciples. We're going to learn about this life relationship with Christ by answering the following four questions: What is a disciple? How do we become a disciple? What is the cost of discipleship? What are the marks of a disciple?

What Is A Disciple?

Before Jesus ascended to heaven, He gave a charge to His followers. We often speak of this charge as "The Great Commission." Jesus spoke these words: "All authority has been given to Me in heaven and on earth. Go therefore and make disciples of all the nations, baptizing them in the name of the Father and of the Son and of the Holy Spirit, teaching them to observe all things that I have commanded you; and lo, I am with you always, even to the end of the age" (Matthew 28:18-20 NKJ).

Jesus said to make disciples (not converts). Of course, before we can make a disciple of someone else, we must first be a disciple ourselves. So what is a disciple? According to the Bible, a disciple is a follower who learns from his teacher in order to imitate his teacher in word, thought and deed. From this definition, we learn that a disciple is a follower, a learner and an imitator. He follows in order to learn and he learns in order to imitate.

Followers

Jesus called people to follow Him. He initially put forth this challenge at the Sea of Galilee. Matthew recorded it for us: "Now Jesus, walking by the Sea of Galilee, saw two brothers, Simon called Peter, and Andrew his brother, casting a net into the sea; for they were fishermen. And He said to them, 'Follow Me, and I will make you fishers of men.' Then they immediately left their nets and followed Him. And going on from there, He saw two other brothers, James the son of Zebedee, and John his brother, in the boat with Zebedee their father, mending their nets. And He called them, and immediately they left the boat and their father, and followed Him' " (Matthew 4:18-22 NKJ).

Luke added that they forsook *all* and followed Him (Luke 5:11).

These men were fishermen. This is how they made their living. It was a family business. I'm sure their father spent many years of hard labor making the business prosperous. He taught his boys how to fish. He had great plans for them. No doubt he was preparing them to take over the business when he retired.

But Jesus had a different plan for their life. His plan was to make them fishers of men (Luke 5:10). He called them to leave the family business and abandon all their dreams, plans, aspirations and personal ambitions. Instead of following their own life plan, they were to follow Him. And I bet daddy wasn't too thrilled about their choice.

Likewise, God has a plan for your life. He makes His plan known to you when you follow Jesus Christ by appropriating Him as your Lord and walking in the Spirit. This is what Jesus meant when He said, "I am the light of the world; he who follows me will not walk in darkness, but will have the light of life" (John 8:12 RSV).

God will give you light to see His divine plan for your life. As He illuminates the pathway, you make whatever adjustments are necessary in your own life-plan to conform it to His. *Fulfilling God's plan for your life becomes your reason for living and gives meaning and purpose to all that you do.*

Adjusting Priorities

Now God has given all of us certain talents and abilities. And usually we have a job where we are able to use these God-given qualities. Normally, God wants you to stay right on the job where He found you. But He wants to use you on that job to be a fisher of men and women. This usually requires that we make some adjustments in our priorities, attitudes and actions.

God probably won't ask you to literally leave your job as He did the first disciples. But He might. You must be willing to follow Him. *But I can assure you that, whatever God asks*

113

you to do, He will first put the desire in your heart to do it.
God's plan will not be some grievous burden for you.
Instead, as God puts the desire in your heart, whatever He
asks you to do will be just what you want to do. You must be
willing to be willing to follow Him. God will do the rest.

Learners

Jesus calls us to follow Him because He leads us to God.
As we listen to His words and observe His life, we learn the
mind, heart and ways of God. God said through the Prophet
Isaiah, "Seek the Lord while he may be found, call upon
Him while he is near; let the wicked forsake his way, and the
unrighteous man his thoughts; let him return to the Lord,
that he may have mercy on him, and to our God, for he will
abundantly pardon. For my thoughts are not your thoughts,
neither are your ways my ways, says the LORD. For as the
heavens are higher than the earth, so are my ways higher
than your ways and my thoughts than your thoughts"
(Isaiah 55:6-9 RSV).

God is not like His human creatures. His character is
different from ours. His ways are different from our ways.
His thoughts are not our thoughts. But He has supremely
revealed Himself to us through Jesus Christ, Who said,
". . . He who has seen Me has seen the Father . . ." (John
14:9 NKJ).

When God raised up Moses as a prophet, He told Moses
that one would come in the future who would be the perfect
prophet, or spokesman, for God. God said to Moses, "I
will raise up for them a prophet like you from among their
brethren; and I will put my words in his mouth, and he shall
speak to them all that I command him. And whoever will not
give heed to my words which he shall speak in my name, I
myself will require it of him" (Deuteronomy 18:18-19 RSV).

Jesus claimed to be this prophet. He said, "He who
believes in Me, believes not in Me but in Him who sent Me.
And he who sees Me sees Him who sent Me. I have come as a
light into the world, that whoever believes in Me should not
abide in darkness. And if anyone hears My words, and does

not believe, I do not judge him; for I did not come to judge the world but to save the world. He who rejects Me, and does not receive My words, has that which judges him—the word that I have spoken will judge him in the last day. For I have not spoken on My own authority; but the Father who sent Me gave Me a command, what I should say and what I should speak. And I know that His command is everlasting life. Therefore, whatever I speak, just as the Father has told Me, so I speak" (John 12:44-50 NKJ).

So we follow Jesus to learn the things of God. He not only gives us God's Word, but He Himself was the Word of God in the flesh. This means that God fully and completely revealed Himself to us through the life and ministry of Jesus Christ. (See John 5:36; 8:18; 14:8-11.)

Renewing Our Minds

As we follow Him, the Holy Spirit will enlighten our minds to help us know God and learn how to walk in His ways. Jesus said, ". . . the Helper, the Holy Spirit, whom the Father will send in My name, He will teach you all things, and bring to your remembrance all things that I said to you" (John 14:26 NKJ).

Jesus also said of the Holy Spirit, "However, when He, the Spirit of truth, has come, He will guide you into all truth; for He will not speak on His own authority, but whatever He hears He will speak; and He will tell you things to come. He will glorify Me, for He will take of what is Mine and declare it to you. All things that the Father has are Mine. Therefore I said that He will take of Mine and declare it to you" (John 16:13-15 NKJ).

We learn the things of God by following Jesus Christ and walking in the Spirit. This is why Paul wrote a verse we've already mentioned: "I beseech you therefore, brethren, by the mercies of God, that you present your bodies a living sacrifice, holy, acceptable to God, which is your reasonable service. And do not be conformed to this world, but be transformed by the renewing of your mind, that you may prove what is that good and acceptable and perfect will of God" (Romans 12:1-2 NKJ).

Imitators

We follow Jesus in order to learn from Jesus. We learn from Jesus in order to *imitate Him*. The word "imitate" means to act like someone else in word, thought and deed.

Children always imitate their father. Sometimes this can be good, but sometimes it can be very embarrassing. As we have just learned, Jesus imitated His heavenly Father. Everything He thought, said and did was in the character of God. This is why God said of Jesus, "This is My beloved Son, in whom I am well pleased" (Matthew 3:17 NKJ).

By Word And Example

Jesus taught His followers in two ways. He taught by word and by example. What He taught by His words, He lived out through His life. Jesus was a walking, living, breathing theological seminary and observatory. *As the disciples heard Jesus teach, they also saw Him demonstrate His teachings through His life.* (See Acts 1:1.) He was the example and role-model after which they were to pattern their own lives. They would be able to do this through the power of the Holy Spirit Who would live the life of Jesus through them. *They, in turn, would be examples for others to follow, learn from and imitate.*

Divine Copycats

Paul often reminded his followers about how he lived before them as an example for them to imitate. He wrote to the Christians at Corinth, "Be imitators of me, as I am of Christ" (1 Corinthians 11:1 RSV).

To the Philippian Christians, he said, "Brethren, join in imitating me, and mark those who so live as you have an example in us" (Philippians 3:17 RSV).

He reminded the Thessalonians with these words, "And you became imitators of us and of the Lord . . ." (1 Thessalonians 1:6 RSV). (See also 2 Thessalonains 3:9.)

116

Paul did not speak this way about himself in a self-righteous "holier-than-thou" attitude. But since he lived out what he taught, he was able, in humility and good conscience, to point to himself as an example for the other Christians to observe.

Furthermore, he encouraged them to also be examples. He wrote to Timothy, "Let no one despise your youth, but be an example to the believers in word, in conduct, in love, in spirit, in faith, in purity" (1 Timothy 4:12 NKJ).

He encouraged the Ephesian Christians with these words, "Therefore be imitators of God, as beloved children" (Ephesians 5:1 RSV).

We too are to teach people about God by sharing with them His Word and living it out before them. We are God's living letters (2 Corinthians 3:1-3). As we walk with God, the Holy Spirit transforms us into the image of Jesus Christ (2 Corinthians 3:18). His life is reproduced in us.

Keeping Your Eyes On Jesus

People need to see examples of the Christian life being lived out before them. They would rather see a sermon than hear one. We instinctively recognize this and often piously tell people to "keep your eyes on Jesus."

But where is Jesus? He is physically in heaven. If people were to look up into the sky to see Him, they wouldn't be able to, unless God gave them some special vision of heaven. *So how are they going to see Jesus? They are going to see Him as He lives out His life on planet earth through His spiritual body, the Church. They are going to see Him as His life is reproduced in you!*

If you are a Christian, how are your friends and acquaintances going to know about God's holiness unless they see it in you? How will they know about God's righteousness unless you live a righteous life before them? How will they know that God is love unless His love is flowing out of you? How will they know that God is good unless they see His goodness in you?

117

Salt And Light

We Christians are the God-containers on planet earth. Jesus lives His life through us. As the life of Christ is reproduced in us by the Holy Spirit, we have two effects on those around us. *Jesus said we would be salt and light.*

Here are His words in Matthew 5:13: "You are the salt of the earth; but if the salt loses its flavor, how shall it be seasoned? It is then good for nothing but to be thrown out and trampled under foot by men" (NKJ).

Our bodies require a certain amount of water in order to remain healthy. If we eat salt, we become thirsty. This creates within us a desire to drink water. Likewise, as the life of Jesus Christ is reproduced in us, it will create within others a thirst and desire to drink of the living waters of life that only Jesus can provide. This will make them healthy spiritually, physically and emotionally.

Jesus went on to say, "You are the light of the world. A city that is set on a hill cannot be hidden. Nor do they light a lamp and put it under a basket, but on a lampstand, and it gives light to all who are in the house. Let your light so shine before men, that they may see your good works and glorify your Father who is in heaven" (Matthew 5:14-16 NKJ).

I pointed out earlier that light has two basic functions, life and sight. The Bible says that without Christ people are dead in their trespasses and sins and are blinded spiritually (Ephesians 2:1, 5; 2 Corinthians 4:4). But when we walk as children of light (Ephesians 5:8) they will see their need for Christ and receive His eternal life as they are born again (from above) by the Holy Spirit.

As we follow Jesus and humbly learn from Him, His life is reproduced in us. Those around us will see that life and want what we have. We then will be able to reproduce that same life in others. May all of us who are believers sincerely and humbly be able to say to our friends and acquaintances, "Imitate me as I imitate Christ."

How Do We Become A Disciple?

The second question we want to answer in this chapter is this: how do we become a disciple? There is really only one requirement, but it is a requirement to which few are willing to commit. *The requirement is self-death.* We must die to our self-life.

The word "self-life" refers to our own personal soulish life-plan. Before we become Jesus' disciple, this life-plan is naturally centered around us rather than Him. It's based on our dreams, our plans, our aspirations and our ambitions. But once we become Jesus' disciple, we're going to follow His plan for our life. And His plan for our life is not going to be the same as our plan. *So, to die to ourselves simply means we willingly lay aside our life-plan for His.*

Jesus, of course, set this example for us. He said, ". . . I have come down from heaven, not to do My own will, but the will of Him who sent Me" (John 6:38 NKJ).

He calls His disciples to do the same. Jesus said to all who would follow Him, "If anyone desires to come after Me, let him deny himself, take up his cross daily, and follow Me. For whoever desires to to save his life will lose it, but whoever loses his life for My sake will save it" (Luke 9:23-24 NKJ).

Jesus spoke about taking up our cross daily. Many people misunderstand what Jesus meant by this. They think He was talking about them having to bear some heavy burden to the point of suffering for Jesus' sake. But this is not at all what He meant.

To understand the meaning of Jesus' words, we must place ourselves in His time period and understand Him as His listeners would have understood Him. If you lived in Jesus' time and saw someone carrying his own cross, you knew that person was going to die. *Likewise, to "take up your cross daily" means to die to yourself.*

Dying To Live

Paul wrote to the Galatian Christians that he was dead to the world and the world was dead to him (Galatians 6:14).

By that, he meant that he no longer cared for his own personal worldly ambitions. He no longer coveted the world's applause, praise, awards, honors and glory. He only coveted the things of God. He only desired to follow Jesus and walk in His divine life-plan. At the same time, the world system no longer cared to honor Paul. As far as it was concerned, Paul was dead.

Paul summarized this self-death requirement in a verse we mentioned in an earlier chapter. He said to these same Galatians, "I have been crucified with Christ; it is no longer I who live, but Christ who lives in me; and the life I now live in the flesh I live by faith in the Son of God, who loved me and gave himself for me" (Galatians 2:20 RSV).

Contribution Or Commitment?

This self-death requirement demands that we commit ourselves completely to the Lordship of Jesus Christ in every area of our lives. *It seems that many professing Christians only desire to make a contribution to the kingdom of God, but they are not willing to really commit their lives to it.* Let me tell you a little story to explain the difference between a contribution and a commitment.

A chicken and a pig were good friends. One day, as they were walking together, the chicken noticed an advertisement in the window of a restaurant. The advertisement read, "Bacon and eggs—all you can eat for $1.00." Feeling somewhat generous, the chicken turned to the pig and said, "Let's go in and make a contribution." To that, the pig replied, "You are only going to make a contribution, but I'll have to make a commitment."

Well, the chicken had in mind laying a few eggs and then going on his own way. But the pig was going to have to give his life. Do you see the difference? Many professing Christians are like the chicken. They only want to make a contribution to the kingdom of God. They lay a few eggs (religious activities) and think they have done their duty and pleased God. But God isn't pleased. He is not interested in our contribution to His Kingdom. He wants us to commit our lives to it. *God doesn't want anything you have—He wants you!* He's not interested in your service for Him but your surrender to Him!

What about you, dear reader? Are you making a contribution or a commitment? Perhaps you have been one who has been content just making contributions to the kingdom of God. But you have never really committed your life to it. It is my prayer that you will make that commitment and give yourself completely to become Jesus' disciple. But as much as I hope you will make that decision, I must first warn you to count the cost that it involves.

What Is The Cost Of Discipleship?

Jesus Himself told us to *count the cost* before becoming His disciple. Luke recorded the following account: "And great multitudes went with Him. And He turned and said to them, 'If anyone comes to Me and does not hate his father and mother, wife and children, brothers and sisters, yes, and his own life also, he cannot be My disciple. And whoever does not bear his cross and come after Me cannot be My disciple' " (Luke 14:25-27 NKJ).

A big crowd was following Jesus. They had seen Him perform many miracles. Many of the people were nothing more than curiosity seekers. Others were following Him for selfish reasons. They just wanted Him to meet their own needs. They weren't really committed to Him.

A Challenge To The Crowd

So Jesus spoke to them about the need for commitment. He looked at that big crowd and knew that the vast majority of the people did not understand the commitment to which He was calling them. Furthermore, He also knew that once they did understand, they would no longer follow Him.

Jesus didn't want them to be misled. *So He told them that whoever followed Him must love Him more than anyone else.* This would include the person's most cherished relationships with his own family members, and even the person's own life as well. Their relationship to Him would be more important than any earthly relationship. This is the meaning of the Greek word that is translated into English as "hate." (See also Matthew 10:34-39.) It was like Jesus was saying to the crowds, "Before you hitch your wagon to me, let's make something very clear. First, count the cost."

Jesus then gave two examples about counting the cost. The first was about a builder, the second a king. He said, ". . . which of you, intending to build a tower, does not sit down first and count the cost, whether he has enough to finish it—lest, after he has laid the foundation, and is not able to finish, all who see it begin to mock him, saying, 'This man begin to build and was not able to finish.' Or what king, going to make war against another king, does not sit down first and consider whether he is able with ten thousand to meet him who comes against him with twenty thousand? Or else, while the other is still a great way off, he sends a delegation and asks conditions of peace" (Luke 14:28-32 NKJ).

In both of these examples, Jesus was teaching the necessity of counting the cost before making a decision. He knew the crowd of would-be followers had not done this concerning their relationship to Him. Now that He had them thinking about it, He quickly made His point, "So likewise, whoever of you does not forsake all that he has cannot be My disciple" (Luke 14:33 NKJ).

The Prosperity Christian

Luke also told us about three who came to Jesus wanting to be His disciples. But they had not counted the cost. Luke wrote about the first man: "Now it happened, as they journeyed on the road, that someone said to Him, 'Lord, I will follow You wherever You go.' And Jesus said to him, 'Foxes have holes and birds of the air have nests, but the son of Man has nowhere to lay His head' " (Luke 9:57-58 NKJ).

This man thought he wanted to follow Jesus. He had heard, no doubt, that Jesus was going to establish a kingdom. He thought this was going to be a physical kingdom. He wanted to be part of this physical kingdom because it would mean material prosperity for him. Jesus pointed out that He had no material prosperity to offer the person. In fact, He didn't even have a house to call His own. He stayed in other people's houses or slept in the open. This man wanted to follow Jesus for what he could get from Him. *He had not counted the cost of material comforts.*

It seems that a lot of people today are like this man. They follow Jesus for what they think He can do for them. They are only interested in themselves. Theirs is a "gimme-gimme" relationship with Jesus. If God doesn't instantly meet their every self-centered demand, their hearts grow cold. They are not prepared for hardships. They are not willing to make sacrifices. They haven't counted the cost of material comforts.

The Self-Sufficient Christian

Now let's consider the second man who came to Jesus. Luke wrote, "Then He said to another, 'Follow Me.' But he said, 'Lord, let me first go and bury my father.' Jesus said to him, 'Let the dead bury their own dead, but you go and preach the kingdom of God' " (Luke 9:59-60 NKJ).

This is an interesting situation. To properly understand this man's concern, we must relate it to Jewish customs and practices that were common during the time of Jesus. One such custom was that the first-born stayed home until his father died. He would then bury his father and receive his inheritance. Then he would be self-sufficient and not have to depend on anyone.

This could very well be the situation with this man. If so, he was telling Jesus that he wanted to wait until he was self-sufficient before he followed Him. In this way, he would have had enough money to take care of himself and not have to depend on anyone, including Jesus.

And you know, there are many Christians like that today. They'll follow Jesus up to a point. But they will never put themselves in a position where they actually have to depend on Him and trust Him. *They are self-sufficient.* They've got their financial security blankets to cover them in times

123

of crisis. They have "In God we trust" written on their money, but it's really their money they have put their trust in. They don't need anyone, including Jesus. They haven't counted the cost of total dependence on God.

The Family Christian

Then there's the third man who came to Jesus. Luke wrote, "And another also said, 'Lord, I will follow You, but let me first go and bid them farewell who are at my house.' But Jesus said to him, 'No one, having put his hand to the plow, and looking back, is fit for the kingdom of God' " (Luke 9:61-62 NKJ).

Now what was this man's problem? His problem was that he was more concerned with what his daddy thought than he was with Jesus' call to follow Him. He wanted to ask his father's permission to follow Jesus. He put his father's authority over Jesus' authority. He did not count the cost of *family rejection*. Therefore, Jesus rejected him.

Many Christians in our modern world have the same problem. They would like to follow Jesus, but not if it's going to cause problems within the family. They are more concerned about their family relationships than about their relationships with God. This becomes a barrier keeping them from being Jesus' disciple.

These are just three representative cases of people who wanted to be Jesus' disciples but had not counted the cost. One was not willing to sacrifice financially. Another wanted to be self-sufficent. The third put his family first. Beloved reader, is there anything that is keeping you from being Jesus' disciple? If there is, I pray that you will count the cost and count His call to discipleship to be the most important consideration in your life. God help you to make that decision.

What Are The Marks Of A Disciple?

We come now to the last question in this chapter: what are the marks of a disciple? Many people claim to be disciples of Jesus Christ, but just saying it doesn't make it a fact.

The person must demonstrate it in his or her life. I believe the Bible teaches *six qualities* in a person's life that mark that person as a true disciple of Jesus Christ. Jesus, as our example, demonstrated these in His own life, and He requires each of His disciples to follow His example. These six qualities are as follows:

Love

The first mark of one who is a disciple of Jesus Christ is *love*. Jesus loved. Paul wrote, "Therefore be imitators of God, as beloved children. And walk in love, as Christ loved us and gave himself up for us, a fragrant offering and sacrifice to God" (Ephesians 5:1-2 RSV).

Jesus said, "A new commandment I give to you, that you love one another; as I have loved you, that you also love one another. By this all will know that you are My disciples, if you have love for one another" (John 13:34-35 NKJ).

The Greek word for love in this verse is *agape*. It is the God-kind of love we learned about in an earlier chapter. *God's kind of love is an uncaused love that has been poured into our hearts by the Holy Spirit.* It enables us to love others unconditionally and includes our enemies as well as our friends.

Jesus said this directive to love was a new commandment. The commandment itself wasn't new because God gave it to the Hebrews fifteen hundred years before. (See Leviticus 19:18, 34.) But what made this commandment new was the quality or type of love with which we would be loving. We would be loving others as Christ has loved us with an unconditional, uncaused sacrificial love.

Jesus said that this agape love is the true mark of His disciples. The Apostle John put it this way: "Beloved, let us love one another, for love is of God; and everyone who loves is born of God and knows God. He who does not love does not know God, for God is love. . . . And we have known and believed the love that God has for us. God is love, and he who abides in love abides in God, and God in Him" (1 John 4:7-8, 16 NKJ).

125

John then added, "If someone says, 'I love God,' and hates his brother, he is a liar; for he who does not love his brother whom he has seen, how can he love God whom he has not seen? And this commandment we have from Him: that he who loves God must love his brother also" (1 John 4:20-21 NKJ).

Many people may say that they love Jesus. Many people may say they love you. But the proof is in their attitude and actions. John put it so well. He said, "My little children, let us not love in word or in tongue, but in deed and in truth" (1 John 3:18 NKJ).

Fruit-Bearing

The second mark of a true disciple of Jesus Christ is that he *bears fruit*. This is the fruit of the Spirit. Jesus bore fruit. In fact, as we have already learned, the fruit of the Spirit is simply the very character and life of Jesus being lived out of us by the Holy Spirit. Thus, fruit-bearing is a true test of a person's relationship with Jesus Christ.

Jesus said it in these words, "I am the true vine, and My Father is the vinedresser. Every branch in Me that does not bear fruit He takes away; and every branch that bears fruit He prunes, that it may bear more fruit. You are already clean because of the word which I have spoken to you. Abide in Me, and I in you. As the branch cannot bear fruit of itself, unless it abides in the vine, neither can you, unless you abide in Me. I am the vine, you are the branches. He who abides in Me and I in him, bears much fruit; for without Me you can do nothing. If anyone does not abide in Me, he is cast out as a branch and is withered; and they gather them and throw them into the fire, and they are burned. If you abide in Me, and My words abide in you, you will ask what you desire, and it shall be done for you. By this My Father is glorified, that you bear much fruit; so you will be My disciples" (John 15:1-8 NKJ).

Jesus then added, "You did not choose Me, but I chose you and appointed you that you should go and bear fruit, and that your fruit should remain . . ." (John 15:16 NKJ).

Jesus warned us against people who profess to be Christians but bear no fruit. His words were, "Beware of false prophets, who come to you in sheep's clothing, but inwardly they are ravenous wolves. You will know them by their fruits. Do men gather grapes from thornbushes or figs from thistles? Even so, every good tree bears good fruit, but a bad tree bears bad fruit. A good tree cannot bear bad fruit, nor can a bad tree bear good fruit. Every tree that does not bear good fruit is cut down and thrown into the fire. Therefore by their fruits you will know them" (Matthew 7:15-20 NKJ).

The test of a disciple of Jesus is not that the person understands everything about the Bible, can debate doctrines of the faith, perform miracles, sing in the choir or teach a Sunday school class. The test is *fruit-bearing.*

Obedience

The third mark or quality of a disciple of Jesus Christ is *obedience.* Jesus obeyed the Father. He said, ". . . I always do those things that please Him" (John 8:29 NKJ). On another occasion, Jesus said, "My food [nourishment] is to do the will of Him who sent Me, and to finish His work" (John 4:34 NKJ).

Jesus expects no less of His disciples. He had been preaching and many believed in Him. But He wanted them to know that *believing must be evidenced by obedience.* So He stopped in the middle of His sermon and said, "If you abide in My word, you are My disciples indeed" (John 8:31 NKJ).

Jesus coupled obedience with love. He told His disciples, "If you love Me, keep My commandments. . . . He who has My commandments and keeps them, it is he who loves Me" (John 14:15, 21 NKJ).

On one occasion, Jesus gave a rebuke. He said, "But why do you call Me 'Lord, Lord,' and do not do the things which I say?" (Luke 6:46 NKJ).

He went on to say, "Not everyone who says to Me, 'Lord, Lord,' shall enter the kingdom of heaven, but he who does the will of My Father in heaven. Many will say to Me in that day, 'Lord, Lord, have we not prophesied in Your name, cast out demons in Your name, and done many wonders in Your name?' And then I will declare to them, 'I never knew you; depart from Me, you who practice lawlessness!' " (Matthew 7:21-23 NKJ).

Jesus then gave them an example to illustrate His point. He said, "Therefore whoever hears these sayings of Mine, and does them, I will liken him to a wise man who built his house on the rock: and the rain descended, the floods came, and the winds blew and beat on that house; and it did not fall, for it was founded on the rock. Now everyone who hears these sayings of Mine, and does not do them, will be like a foolish man who built his house on the sand: and the rain descended, the floods came, and the winds blew and beat on that house; and it fell. And great was its fall" (Matthew 7:24-27 NKJ).

The Word of God is not just to be learned; it is to be obeyed. If we really love God and want to follow Jesus, we will learn what He wants us to do and then we will do it. Not everyone who sings "He is Lord" is a disciple of Jesus. Not everyone who attends church or goes to a Bible study is a disciple of Jesus. A disciple of Jesus Christ obeys Jesus Christ. As the Apostle James wrote, "Be ye doers of the word, and not hearers only . . ." (James 1:22 KJV).

Submission

A disciple of Jesus Christ also *submits to Jesus Christ.* Submission is different from obedience. Obedience refers to outward acts. Submission relates to heart attitudes. A person can be obedient and not submissive. He can perform an outward act but do it with a hard heart. On the other hand, he can be submissive and not obedient. This would be a situation in which a person must refuse to obey an ungodly instruction, but would do so with a humble spirit. *A disciple is both obedient and submissive to the Lordship of Jesus Christ.* He not only obeys, but he does so joyfully from his heart.

Jesus submitted to His heavenly Father. The night Jesus was taken captive, He was agonizing over the events He was soon to face. Not only was He going to be beaten unmercifully, profoundly humiliated and crucified, but, even worse, for the first time in all eternity, He was going to be separated from His heavenly Father. Yet He prayed, "O My Father, if it is possible, let this cup pass from Me; nevertheless, not as I will, but as You will" (Matthew 26:39 NKJ).

Jesus not only obeyed, but He joyfully submitted to the will of His heavenly Father. As our example, the writer of Hebrews says we should be "looking unto Jesus, the author and finisher of our faith, who for the joy that was set before Him endured the cross, despising the shame, and has sat down at the right hand of the throne of God" (Hebrews 12:2 NKJ).

Regarding submission, Jesus said, "Come to Me, all you who labor and are heavy laden, and I will give you rest. Take My yoke upon you and learn from Me, for I am gentle and lowly in heart, and you will find rest for your souls. For My yoke is easy and My burden is light" (Matthew 11:28-30 NKJ).

The yoke was used to couple two things together. In ancient times it was placed on the necks of the conquered, showing their servitude to their new masters (Jeremiah 27:2; 28:13). It was a sign of submission to authority.

We who have been coupled to Jesus Christ by the Holy Spirit are to submit to His authority over our lives. It takes many Christians a lifetime to realize that Jesus is more than just our friend who desires to bless us and help us out when we get in trouble. Some Christians never realize this. *Jesus came to take over our lives.* Our relationship to Him is one of Lord and servant. He is the master, ruler and controller of our life. Therefore, we submit to His authority, joyfully doing those things that please Him.

Christ's authority is supreme. Jesus said in Matthew 28:18 that He had been given all authority and power. Yet, in the church, He delegates this authority to those He places in positions of leadership. *We submit to Christ through our spiritual leaders.*

The writer of Hebrews said, "Obey those who rule over you, and be submissive, for they watch out for your souls, as those who must give account. Let them do so with joy and not with grief, for that would be unprofitable for you" (Hebrews 13:17 NKJ).

Many Christians want to be in positions of authority. But they are not willing to submit to authority. *They think they are "free spirits" who can do their own thing and need no one but Jesus to tell them what to do.* This sounds so spiritual—but it's not. Jesus guides us directly but also through our spiritual leaders as they speak the Word of God to our lives.

This does not mean blind obedience. All relationships are "as unto the Lord." God never expects us to obey an instruction that is contrary to Scripture. But He does expect us to have a submissive spirit, even if we're not able to obey an instruction that we know is not from God. Remember: God is interested in our heart attitudes, as well as our outward acts.

So we must learn to receive authority before we can exercise it. We must learn to take orders before we can give them. We do this by submitting to the God-given authority of our spiritual leaders. If at all possible, *every disciple of Jesus Christ should be attached to a local expression of the body of Christ and in submission to its leaders.* This is how we submit to Christ's authority in our lives.

Servanthood

Another mark of a disciple of Jesus Christ is *servanthood.* Jesus served. At the last supper Jesus had with His disciples, they had been arguing over who was going to be the greatest in His kingdom. Jesus needed some dramatic way to demonstrate that the road to greatness was through servanthood. So He rose from His place at the head of the table, took off His master's robe, put on a towel, which was the dress of a servant, and washed their feet. That ended the argument as they were all stunned and silenced by Jesus' act.

After Jesus washed their feet, He said, "You call me Teacher and Lord, and you say well, for so I am. If I then, your Lord and Teacher, have washed your feet, you also ought to wash one another's feet. For I have given you an example, that you should do as I have done to you. Most assuredly, I say to you, a servant is not greater than his master; nor is he who is sent greater than he who sent him. If you know these things, happy are you if you do them"(John 13:13-17 NKJ).

One day James and John's mother came to Jesus and asked Him to let her sons have special places of rule and authority in His kingdom. Well, the other disciples heard her and got mad. How could she ask such a thing, they thought? Jesus heard them arguing and used the situation to teach them how one comes to rule in the kingdom of God.

Matthew wrote, "But Jesus called them to Himself and said, 'You know that the rulers of the Gentiles lord it over them, and those who are great exercise authority over them. Yet it shall not be so among you; but whoever desires to become great among you, let him be your servant. And whoever desires to be first among you, let him be your slave—just as the Son of Man did not come to be served, but to serve, and to give His life a ransom for many" (Matthew 20:25-28 NKJ).

On another occasion, Jesus told the religious leaders, ". . . he who is greatest among you shall be your servant. And whoever exalts himself will be abased, and he who humbles himself will be exalted" (Matthew 23:11-12 NKJ).

The way to greatness in the kingdom of God is through servanthood. In fact, a disciple of Jesus Christ exercises his spiritual authority through serving. We Christians often speak about the freedom and liberty we have through Christ. I sometimes hear Christian friends quoting Galatians 5:1 where Paul wrote, "Stand fast therefore in the liberty by which Christ has made us free, and do not be entangled again with a yoke of bondage" (NKJ).

Christ has set us free and this is fantastic. It's wonderful to be free in Jesus. But why has He set us free? Paul answered this question for us in the same chapter to the Galatian Christians. He said, "For you, brethren, have been called to liberty; only do not use liberty as an opportunity for the flesh, but through love serve one another" (Galatians 5:13 NKJ).

Paul reminded us of the purpose for which Christ has set us free. He has freed us from ourselves that we, through love, might serve others. As we serve others in Christ's body, we are actually serving Him. This is another reason why it is important to be physically attached to the local expression of His body. We exercise our authority in the local church by serving the members of that local church. In this way we serve Christ.

This is a privilege God has given us. Jesus set the example. He expects us to follow that example and spiritually wash the feet of our Christian brothers and sisters by serving them in love. This is not only our privilege, it's our duty. It is the true mark of a disciple.

Jesus said it this way, "Will any one of you, who has a servant plowing or keeping sheep, say to him when he has come in from the field, 'Come at once and sit down at table'? Will he not rather say to him, 'Prepare supper for me, and gird yourself and serve me, till I eat and drink; and afterward you shall eat and drink'? Does he thank the servant because he did what was commanded? So you also, when you have done all that is commanded you, say, 'We are unworthy servants; we have only done what was our duty' " (Luke 17:7-10 RSV).

Reproduction

The last mark or quality of a disciple of Jesus Christ is *reproduction*. Jesus reproduced His life in others. Jesus' followers were anxiously waiting for Him to establish His kingdom. As the time drew near, Jesus said, "The hour has come that the Son of Man should be glorified. Most assuredly, I say to you, unless a grain of wheat falls into the ground and dies, it remains alone; but if if dies, it produces much grain. He who loves his life will lose it, and he who hates his life in this world will keep it for eternal life" (John 12:23-25 NKJ).

Jesus' followers expected Him to overthrow the Roman Empire by force and establish a political kingdom on planet earth. He is going to do this at His second coming. *But the purpose of His first coming was to overthrow the kingdom of self that is within each of us and establish His rule in our hearts.* His objective was to bring us forgiveness for our sins and reproduce His life in us. But He had to die in order to do it.

Since Jesus lived a perfect life and never knew sin, it was not necessary for Him to die. He could have bypassed the cross and ascended back to heaven. But He would have gone alone. He would have showed up empty-handed. He would not have accomplished His objective.

So as He spoke about entering into His glory, He also talked about dying. He was the "grain of wheat" that would fall to the ground and die. But because He never knew sin, death couldn't hold Him in the grave. Therefore He came forth victorious over death, walked planet earth for forty days and appeared to many of His followers. Then He ascended back to heaven from where He sent the Holy Spirit to give us eternal life and reproduce His own life in us.

Jesus then said we are to follow His example of self-death in order to reproduce His life in others. He said those who love their life will lose it. The Greek word that is translated into this English word life is *psuche*. It refers to our soulish self-life which is basically our old Adam-like nature seeking to do its own thing. As long as we try to hold on to this life, the life of Christ will not be produced in us nor reproduced in others. Furthermore, we'll lose this life in the end as God brings down all that is opposed to Him.

But to those who prefer not their psuche life, Jesus promises that they will have eternal life. The Greek word which is translated into this English word "life" is *zoe*. This refers to the life of Jesus Christ coming to live in us through the Holy Spirit. It's the God-kind of life in the Spirit which we have been learning about in this book.

133

As we die to ourselves, the Holy Spirit lives the life of Jesus Christ in us. This life flows out of us towards others who will also want to receive Christ in them. In this way, we reproduce His life in those around us. They then become the disciple of Jesus in us. *We don't just bring them to Christ and leave them.* But we give ourselves to them as Jesus gave Himself to us. We commit our life to them as He committed His life to us. (See 1 Thessalonians 2:8.) We teach them by word and example and by so doing we say to them, "Follow, learn and imitate Christ in me."

This is what it means to live as Christ's disciple. We follow Him, learn from Him and imitate Him. His love flows out of us. We bear the fruit of His Spirit. We obey Him and submit to His authority. We serve Him. We die to ourselves so that His life might be reproduced through us in others. *We don't do this in isolation but through relationships that God has established between us and others in a local Christian community. As we live unto them, we are living unto Him.*

A Final Word

We come now to the end of this book. But I hope it's just the beginning of an exciting life for you with Christ in heavenly places. May God help you to know who you are in Christ. Realize your identification with Him, appropriate His Lordship and walk in the Spirit. Be filled always with the Holy Spirit for power to minister His life to others. Put on the whole armor of God and stand in the victory Jesus has won for you. Live as Christ's disciple reproducing His life in others. For Jesus said, ". . . *I have come that they may have life* [zoe], *and that they may have it more abundantly*"(John 10:10 NKJ).

Review Exercise 7

1. Give a definition of the word "disciple."

2. What is the requirement to be a disciple of Jesus Christ? Explain!

3. What is the cost of discipleship?

4. List the six marks or qualities of a disciple of Jesus Christ.

    a.

    b.

    c.

    d.

    e.

    f.

5. How can you apply this knowlege to your life?

BIBLE STUDY MATERIALS BY RICHARD BOOKER

BOOKS

For additional copies of this or other books by Richard Booker, order through your local bookstore or clip and mail the Order Form which is provided on the last page of this book following the tape list.

Richard's books can best be described as foundational books written in clear, easy-to-understand language and readable format for practical Christian living. They may be read or studied for deeper understanding of the Bible. They are primarily written for Christians of all levels of maturity but are appropriate for anyone seeking to know God. The following is a list of Richard's other books.

THE MIRACLE OF THE SCARLET THREAD

This book explains how the Old and New Testaments are woven together by the scarlet thread of the blood covenant to tell one complete story throughout the Bible.

COME AND DINE

This book takes the mystery and confusion out of the Bible. It provides background information on how we got the Bible, a survey of every book in the Bible and how each relates to Jesus Christ, practical principles, forms and guidelines for your own personal Bible study and a systematic plan for effectively reading, studying and understanding the Bible for yourself.

INTIMACY WITH GOD

This book is about the God of the Bible. It shows the ways in which God has revealed Himself to us and explains the attributes, plans and purposes of God. Then each attribute is related practically to the reader. This book takes you into the very heart of God and demonstrates how to draw near to Him.

BIBLE STUDY WORKSHOP

Richard developed and teaches a one-day workshop called *Come and Dine*. In this workshop, he teaches Christians how to study the Bible for themselves. Each participant receives a 95-page workbook which he or she will use as a lifetime Bible study reference aid. For a free brochure describing the workshop, check the appropriate box on the Order Form which is provided on the last page of this book following the tape list.

AUDIO CASSETTE TAPE ALBUMS

A list of Richard's teaching cassettes is included on the following pages. All tape series come in an attractive album for your convenience. To order tapes, check the appropriate box on the Order Form which is provided on the last page of this book, then clip and mail.

TAPE LIST

■ *The Bible Series*
BL1 Uniqueness Of The Bible
BL2 How The Books Became The Book
BL3 Survey of Old Testament
BL4 Survey of New Testament
BL5 How We Got Our English Bible
BL6 Getting Into The Bible
BL7 How To Study The Bible
BL8 How To Understand The Bible

■ *Getting To Know God—1*
KG1 Knowing God
KG2 The Self-Existing One
KG3 The Personal Spirit
KG4 The Trinity

■ *Getting To Know God—2*
KG1 God Is Sovereign
KG2 God Is All Power
KG3 God Is All Knowledge
KG4 God Is Everywhere Present
KG5 God Never Changes

■ *Getting To Know God—3*
KG1 God Is Holy
KG2 God Is Love
KG3 God Is Just
KG4 God Is Good

■ *Blood Covenant Series*
BC1 The Blood Covenant
BC2 What Was It Abraham Believed
BC3 The Tabernacle
BC4 The Sacrifices
BC5 The High Priest
BC6 The Passover

■ *Abundant Life Series*
AL1 Knowing Your Dominion
AL2 Identifying With Christ
AL3 Appropriating His Lordship
AL4 Walking in the Spirit
AL5 Ministering in the Spirit
AL6 Wearing the Armor

■ *The Church Series*
CH1 The Church
CH2 The Body of Christ
CH3 Gifts of the Spirit
CH4 Equipping the Saints
CH5 Work of the Ministry
CH6 Building Up the Body

■ *Christian Family Series*
CF1 God's Purpose for Family
CF2 The Husband's Role
CF3 The Wife's Role
CF4 Parent & Children Roles

■ *Faith & Healing Series*
FH1 Divine Healing Today
FH2 Basis For Claiming Healing
FH3 Barriers To Healing

■ *End Time Series*
ET1 Coming World Events—1
ET2 Coming World Events—2
ET3 Judgment Of Christians
ET4 Seven-Year Tribulation
ET5 Second Coming Of Christ
ET6 Millennium
ET7 Great White Throne Judgment
ET8 New Heaven & New Earth

■ *The Feasts Series*
FE1 Passover
FE2 Unleavened Bread
FE3 Pentecost
FE4 Trumpets
FE5 Atonement
FE6 Tabernacles

■ *Sacrifices Series*
SF1 Sin Offering
SF2 Trespass Offering
SF3 Burnt Offering
SF4 Meal Offering
SF5 Peace Offering

■ *Ephesians Series*
EP1 Background & Blessing
EP2 Prayer For Enlightenment
EP3 New Life In Christ
EP4 Who Is The Seed Of Abraham?
EP5 Prayer For Enablement
EP6 Christian Unity
EP7 Ministering To The Saints
EP8 Ministry Of The Saints
EP9 Shedding The Graveclothes
EP10 Imitating The Father
EP11 God's Order For Family
EP12 Spiritual Warfare

■ *Philippians Series*

PH1	Background & Prayer
PH2	Victory In Tribulation
PH3	Keys To Unity
PH4	Honoring One Another
PH5	True Righteousness
PH6	Going On With God
PH7	Standing Together
PH8	Sufficiency Of God

■ *Colossians Series*

CO1	Background
CO2	Person & Work Of Christ
CO3	Christ In You
CO4	Sufficiency Of Christ
CO5	Christ Our Life
CO6	New Man In Christ
CO7	Christ In The Home
CO8	Christ Outside The Home

■ *Thessalonians Series*

TH1	Background & Prayer
TH2	A Winning Defense
TH3	A Welcome Report
TH4	Walking To Please God
TH5	The Day Of The Lord
TH6	Background & Prayer
TH7	Day Of The Lord Again
TH8	No Bums Allowed

■ *Single Messages (Circle On Order Form)*

SM1	Why God Had To Become Man
SM2	Who Was That God Begat
SM3	Feasts Of The Lord
SM4	Philemon
SM5	Lord's Prayer
SM6	Handling Worry
SM7	Knowing God's Will
SM8	Spiritual Leprosy
SM9	Praying In The Name
SM10	Bible Baptisms
SM11	Signs Of His Coming
SM12	Times Of The Gentiles
SM13	Christian Giving
SM14	Master Theme Of Bible
SM15	The Dominant Force
SM16	Personal Testimony
SM17	Call To Discipleship
SM18	Where Are the Dead?

ORDER FORM

Ordering Instructions

To order books and tapes, check the appropriate spaces, then clip and mail the coupon below to **SOUNDS OF THE TRUMPET, INC., 8230 BIRCHGLENN, HOUSTON, TX 77070.**

☐ Please send me _____ copy(ies) of THE MIRACLE OF THE SCARLET THREAD. I have enclosed $6.95 contribution for each copy ordered (price includes shipping).

☐ Please send me _____ copy(ies) of COME AND DINE. I have enclosed $6.95 contribution for each copy ordered (price includes shipping).

☐ Please send me _____ copy(ies) of INTIMACY WITH GOD. I have enclosed $6.95 contribution for each copy ordered (price includes shipping).

☐ Please send me _____ copy(ies) of RADICAL CHRISTIAN LIVING. I have enclosed $6.95 contribution for each copy ordered (price includes shipping).

☐ Please send me _____ copy(ies) of SEATED IN HEAVENLY PLACES. I have enclosed $6.95 contribution for each copy ordered (price includes shipping).

☐ Please send me _____ copy(ies) of BLOW THE TRUMPET IN ZION. I have enclosed $6.95 contribution for each copy ordered (price includes shipping).

☐ Please send me _____ copy(ies) of JESUS IN THE FEASTS OF ISRAEL. I have enclosed $6.95 contribution for each copy ordered (price includes shipping).

☐ Please send me a free brochure describing your workshop on how to study the Bible.

☐ Please send me the following tapes. I have enclosed a $5.00 contribution for each tape ordered (price includes shipping).

☐ Foreign order please include an extra $2.00 for surface postage.

☐ The Bible Series	($32.00)	☐ The Feasts Series	($24.00)
☐ Getting To Know God—1	($16.00)	☐ The Sacrifices Series	($20.00)
☐ Getting To Know God—2	($20.00)	☐ Love Notes From Jesus	($28.00)
☐ Getting To Know God—3	($16.00)	☐ Ephesians Series	($48.00)
☐ Blood Covenant Series	($24.00)	☐ Philippians Series	($32.00)
☐ Abundant Life Series	($24.00)	☐ Colossians Series	($32.00)
☐ The Church Series	($24.00)	☐ Thessalonians Series	($32.00)
☐ The Christian Family	($16.00)	☐ Single Messages (Circle)	
☐ Faith & Healing Series	($12.00)	(SM1 2 3 4 5 6 7 8 9 10 11 12,	
☐ End-Times Series	($32.00)	13 14 15 16 17 18)	($4.00 each)

Name _____

Street _____

City _____

State _____ ZIP _____

Toy:
Pg 6'